Takeovers and the Theory of the Firm

An Empirical Analysis for the United Kingdom 1957–1969

DOUGLAS KUEHN

First published 1975 *by*

THE MACMILLAN PRESS LTD
London and Basingstoke
Associated companies in New York
Dublin, Melbourne, Johannesburg and Madras

SBN 333 15744 3

Printed in Great Britain by
J. W. ARROWSMITH LTD
Winterstoke Road, Bristol, England

Takeovers and the Theory of the Firm

Contents

Appendix

Appendix

takeovers and mergers, unsuccessful takeover bids and defensive strategies employed by firms under offer, and the timing of the offer and its relation to the acquired firm's accounting period. This first aspect of the inquiry will not only present the most complete record of takeover activity during the period and as such will be of interest to a wide spectrum of observers, but also will attempt to examine the usually ignored participant of the takeover, namely the acquired firm.

The second aim of this paper is to develop a theoretical model of takeovers and test it with reference to the data collected. Thus not only will what has happened be described, but I shall attempt to discover why it has happened to particular firms and not others. The methodology adopted will differ from most of the previous investigations into the takeover phenomenon in so far as the emphasis and conclusions rely neither on the purely descriptive survey method nor on the case study method. Neither of these research approaches is invalid as long as conclusions with the first are accepted as possibly misleading generalisations and with the second are limited to the small number of firms studied.

The descriptive survey approach usually incorporates a number of issues relating to takeovers including: changes in concentration, monopoly and the public interest; bidding techniques, strategies and defensive strategies; the financing of takeovers; and taxation and legal considerations. There are a number of books which deal with these and other aspects of takeovers* and since the scope of this study must necessarily be limited, I shall consider the above only indirectly in so far as it relates to the causes of takeovers. This sort of approach is valuable in that it provides necessary background information which leads to an understanding of the climate and way in which takeovers occur. It also indicates likely fruitful areas of research by suggesting factors which may be important in explaining what influences whether or not a firm is taken over. This is its virtue but also its shortcoming; for by sole reliance on this approach one can go no further in explaining the causes of takeovers.

---

* These include Bull and Vice (1958), Cook and Cohen (1958), Mennel (1962), Moon (1968), Stacey (1966), and Reid (1968).

Introduction

Previous research into the field of takeovers and mergers, with several notable exceptions, has suffered both from the lack of an appropriate theoretical structure and consequently, as I shall argue below, misplaced emphasis, as well as weak statistical methodology which has caused many misleading and often incorrect conclusions to be drawn. It is only recently that researchers have attempted to examine takeovers as an aspect of firm behaviour whereas previously they were regarded primarily in the light of the workings of the market mechanism. The emphasis placed upon market pressures as an explanation of takeovers tended, at least in part, to ignore the firm's role in takeover activity. Furthermore, the empirical examination of this activity has consequently been concentrated on its effects at the industry level rather than its causes at the firm level; also, the analysis generally has been insufficient to demonstrate what has occurred, or, what would be more important, why it has occurred.

The purpose of this inquiry is threefold. I shall first set down the record of takeover activity in the UK over the period 1957–69. For this purpose a census of all public quoted companies exclusive of several industry groups has been undertaken and data on a number of financial and stock market variables collected for each of the 3566 firms in the population for each year.* Such a description as the possession of this data makes possible will embody an analysis of the following: the frequency of takeovers through time, the differences between industries in the takeover rate, the method of payment and the bid premium, the characteristics of acquiring firms or raiders, the performance of taken over and non-taken over firms, the distinction between

---

* A full description of the census population and the data collection procedures appear in Appendix I.

Acknowledgements

When I first started my study of UK takeovers I was a Ph.D. student at the University of Warwick researching under the supervision of Professor Keith Cowling and during his brief absence, Professor F. G. Pyatt. I wish to express my particular thanks to Professor Cowling for his encouragement and advice throughout this entire period of research.

The work of data collection was facilitated by the friendly and helpful attitude of the staff of Extel Statistical Services Ltd. I am grateful also to the staff of the University of Warwick Computer Unit for putting the quantity of data thus collected into a state that could be assimilated by the Warwick computer.

The Ph.D. thesis was finally completed in the summer of 1972 by which time I was at the University of Stirling working as a lecturer in the Department of Economics and as a Research Fellow in the Institute of Finance and Investment. My thanks are due to this latter institution for the assistance and support provided.

It was suggested to me at this stage that the thesis would provide a good basis for a book and this present volume is the result of the revisions to my thesis which I accordingly undertook. In this connection I should like to thank the following friends and colleagues: Robin Marris, John Cable, Dick Davies, Colin Day and Andrew Bain. Of course any errors are solely attributable to the author.

D. A. K.

Appendix I

Appendix II

FIGURES

List of Tables and Figures

TABLES

The case study approach, apart from revealing the intricacies of the internal structure of the firms examined, has little to contribute to an understanding of the factors influencing other takeovers because of the absence of any theoretical yardstick. Without such theoretical terms of reference, which this study seeks to identify, conclusions from the case study approach are necessarily limited to the firm or firms involved in the investigation. When a yardstick has been made available, however, it is possible for the case study technique to come into its own. The firms investigated must no longer be studied in isolation but rather can be viewed as deviations from the mean of the population, thereby rendering the conclusions of greater general significance. Thus the present study is aimed at filling the methodological gap created between the two paths of research.

The approach adopted here is to set out the causal hypotheses of takeovers at the firm level and then to develop a testable model of takeovers. Multiple regression techniques will be employed to examine the causes of takeovers within industry classifications. We shall also employ the technique of probit analysis to examine similar hypotheses using all firms' data taken together.

The third aim of this study is to attempt to relate the takeover phenomenon to the recent developments in the theory of the firm. Until recently, takeovers have been examined primarily at the industry level, whereby the effect of takeovers on market structure and takeovers as an aspect of market conduct and performance were considered. Furthermore, takeovers were viewed as a means of achieving the 'optimal' size, or exceeding it, whereby discussion was lead to the analysis of oligopoly and monopoly models. Interest seemed to settle on more normative questions of the social desirability of large firms which possess significant market power. Both in this country and abroad where the takeover boom of the fifties was felt, governments were prompted to reassess their existing controls in the light of this historically unprecedented takeover activity. The economist's role in all this was confined to rather weak statements concerning the abuses or 'evils' of monopoly and the compiling of accounts and comparisons of the legal and institutional treatment of companies which have become large through acquisitions. Throughout, the assumption made by economists was that takeovers were undertaken solely for profit, whether achieved through the realisation of scale economies or increased market power.

In the late fifties and early sixties dissatisfaction was expressed with this assumption of profit maximisation. In part the attack was based on the inability of the classical model of the theory of the firm based on profit maximisation to explain or account for the nature of various observed economic phenomenon such as takeovers, as well as the belief that in the modern corporation where ownership and control were separated, the assumption that managers would act to maximise profits for the owners rather than their own utility directly was unrealistic. The classical model's inability to explain the takeover boom of the fifties was due to several aspects of the nature of the activity. First, it was international, occurring in a number of countries simultaneously; second, its sheer magnitude could not be accounted for by the desire to achieve scale economies especially since other evidence appeared to the effect that, with the exception of several industries, the 'optimal' scale had been reached and exceeded;* third, the harsher governmental controls of monopoly introduced and applied both in this country and abroad had reasonably precluded the possibility of achieving, maintaining and utilising excessive monopoly power; fourth, it emerged that large firms, and by implication those firms undertaking takeovers, did not seem to be more profitable than smaller non-acquiring firms;† finally there was the emergence in the sixties of conglomerates, whose takeover activity had the possibility neither of economies of scale nor of monopoly profits, and which have since demonstrated generally poor performance. All this, while not necessarily conflicting with the idea of long-run profit maximisation, was neither predictable nor explicable in terms of the classical model.

A number of attempts have been made to reformulate the theory of the firm. Most notable among them are the works of W. J. Baumol (1959), Robin Marris (1964) and Oliver Williamson (1964). While each attributes different behavioural objectives to management, they all shared a common starting point.

* See Johnston (1960).
† See Singh and Whittington (1968).

It was the explicit recognition of the separation of ownership and control typified in the modern public company. To the extent that shareholding is disperse, owners will find difficulties (costs) involved in attempts to induce managers to maximise the profits (wealth) accruing to the shareholders. This is seen as a condition for the existence of managerial discretion and hence an explanation for the departure from the traditional assumption that the firm (and by implication the managers as employees) will seek to maximise the profits to the owners. Interest and debate has continued as to the nature of the managerial motivations to be specified in their objective function.* It is unlikely, however, that the debate will ever finally be resolved for two reasons. First, many of the proposals are very similar (e.g. Baumol's sales maximisation and Marris's growth maximisation) so that few, if any, distinct predictions could emerge which could be empirically tested.† That is, there is no direct way to test the objectives of managers,‡ only the predictions which the various hypothesised objective functions generate. Second, it is unlikely that within such a heterogeneous group as the company sector there even exists a single appropriate objective which managers would seek. Thus, having specified managerial discretion in terms of a utility function, it is likely the ingredients would not only be numerous and competing but also subject to external constraints imposed by the owners through the stock market. The operational managerial objective could not only vary between firms due to differences in owner control but also could change through time as circumstances altered within the firm, the industry or even the economy.

Despite the difficulties involved in the generalising of managerial objectives I shall examine in chapter 6 the predictions derivable from the managerial approach to the theory of the firm for takeover raiders, using Marris's growth maximisation

---

* A useful summary of the debate appears in Singh)1971) pp. 6–10.
† This point has been stressed by Baldwin (1964).
‡ An attempt was made recently by Newbould (1970) to uncover the motives behind takeovers by questioning the managers who undertake them. This methodology suffers from those of the case study approach described above as well as the necessity of relying on the managers to reply accurately.

hypothesis as my model. These predictions will be contrasted to those of a profit maximising model in order to see whether it is possible to derive distinct predictions for the two and if so to see which is empirically the more appropriate.

In addition to considering the implications takeovers have for managerial objectives, possibly a more general view of the managerial revisions may be gained by examining the constraints on managerial discretion.* Such constraints have been incorporated into a security variable in the managerial objective function. This desire for security which competes with the attainment of the managerial objective(s) stems mainly from two sources. Firstly, it reflects the existence of the threat of owner sanction, which (at the extreme) will imply a loss of job, or more moderately a possible curtailment in the manager's power to divert resources away from the owners (e.g. the removal of slack). This will depend on the degree of departure from the profit maximising position and the dispersion of shareholding which reflects the difficulties involved in employing such a sanction.

Secondly, there is an externally imposed security constraint operating through the stock market value of the company because of the fear of takeover and consequential loss of job.† The achievement of an objective which results in a departure from the profit maximising position will adversely affect the market valuation of the company and hence lead to an increase in the likelihood of takeover. The impact of this source of the security constraint is dependent again on the extent of the departure from the profit maximising position (i.e. the extent to which attempts to achieve the objective results in a fall in the market valuation) as well as the transaction costs involved in the acquisition of one firm by another. There may be other factors which affect the impact of this constraint such as the defensive position of the firm and the manager's ability to move quickly back towards the profit maximising position and

* Baldwin (1964) has suggested this and Encarcion (1964) investigated the effect on the firm's choices of specifying constraints for use in a lexicographic utility function.

† Singh (1971) pp. 148–9 finds that with a sample of forty-five takeovers approximately 50 per cent of the directors of the acquired company were dismissed within two years of the takeover.

thereby raise the market valuation. At the extreme, the pursuit of an objective which directly competes with profitability may result, instead of takeover, in bankruptcy, which has an even more certain effect on managerial security.

A major part of this study is to investigate the nature and existence of such an inverse relationship between the market valuation and the probability of takeover because of its implications on managerial security and hence the new theories of the firm. Heavy reliance will be placed on the work of Robin Marris (1964) who not only viewed the security constraint upon the managerial objective of growth maximisation in terms of the threat of takeover but also develops a theory of takeover based upon the market valuation of the firm. I shall elaborate on his theory in chapter 2 when a testable model of takeovers will be developed.

Before embarking on this study of a census of UK public companies, I ran a pilot study on a random sample of 250 UK companies designed to reveal the problems likely to be encountered in the data collection, formulation and testing for the existence of this valuation-takeover relationship.* A highly significant relationship with fairly low explanatory power was found. This gave rise to the hope that with an expanded population, additional variables, improved specification of the variables, stratified sampling at the industry level and more rigorous testing procedure, the nature of the valuation-takeover relationship and the takeover mechanism could be more fully exposed.

Subsequent to the publication of the results of this pilot study Ajit Singh (1971) examined the relationship between the market valuation and other financial variables and takeovers. He employed data on a sample of 2126 UK public quoted companies for the period 1948–60 to examine mainly the characteristics of taken over and non-taken over firms. In addition to differences in the composition of the companies examined, the time period, and the emphasis placed on industry analysis in this study, Singh relies primarily on discriminant analysis as his method of testing various hypotheses about takeovers. Nevertheless, where meaningful comparisons can be

* See Kuehn (1969).

drawn between the results of Singh's study and this, reference will be made.

The scope of this study will be limited to the three aims described above because of the enormity of the general subject of takeovers. As stated earlier, the components of a descriptive survey approach to the subject* are only touched upon. A dynamic formulation of the model and the exploration of the desirability or otherwise of takeover activity at its present levels have been omitted entirely but nevertheless remain possibilities for further research. Some discussion of the takeover activity overtime, however, will appear in chapter 1.

---

* See p. 2 above.

1 The Record of Takeover Activity

1.1 INTRODUCTION

It is the primary purpose of this chapter to describe and analyse a number of aspects of the takeover activity that occurred during the period 1 January 1957 to 31 December 1969. This will also serve to acquaint the reader with the climate surrounding this historically unprecedented level of takeovers in order that an appreciation of the theoretical model developed in the next chapter may be gained.

1.2 THE FREQUENCY OF TAKEOVERS AND THE PROBABILITY OF SURVIVAL

In the thirteen year period under study there were 1554 takeovers of public quoted UK companies or 43·42 per cent of the 3566 companies in the census population. This represented net assets of acquired companies of £6837·855 million, and a market value of £13,154·398 million. By comparison with Singh's data for the thirteen year period 1948–60 there were only 461 takeovers out of his sample of 1844 companies or exactly 25 per cent of the total. However, 405 of these occurred during the period 1954–60.* Thus it appears as though the wave of takeover activity of the sixties had its beginnings some time after the mid-fifties. Indeed, Singh indicates with the use of Board of Trade data, that both in terms of the number and value of takeovers the boom appeared to take-off in 1959–60.†

A more complete picture of the frequency of takeovers during the boom is offered by table 1.1. It shows the annual number, book value, and market value of assets acquired during 1957–

* Singh (1971) p. 23.
† Singh (1971) p. 38.

69. Book value in column II is measured as the net assets of the acquired firms and market value (column III) is the value on the stock market of the acquired firms' voting shares after all bidding had been reflected in the price of the firms' shares. These latter two indices of frequency will tend to overstate the value of the taken over firms to the extent that minority interests remain (i.e. not all shares are acquired at the time of the offer). Nevertheless, typically minority interests are acquired at a later date so that this bias would only be evident in the last few years. In any case, since the emergence of the City Code on Takeovers and Mergers in 1968, minority interests have tended to be rapidly acquired following the Code's recommendations. The market value indicator will at the same time underestimate the size of the transaction in that preference shares, debentures, non-voting shares, etc. were excluded. This bias is likely to be significant so that the magnitude of the boom is even greater

TABLE 1.1

Annual Frequency of Takeovers

Year	I No. of takeovers	II Book value of takeovers	III Market value of takeovers	IV Extel Index
1957	76	127·509	117·556	107·7
1958	83	194·281	190·696	104·6
1959	138	253·180	363·256	148·4
1960	107	298·555	473·959	180·9
1961	113	335·172	678·664	194·8
1962	98	244·660	399·645	194·0
1963	90	216·096	392·786	210·0
1964	112	290·032	438·341	222·9
1965	100	466·582	710·396	215·4
1966	89	386·832	566·871	221·8
1967	144	1060·992	1701·564	237·0
1968	240	1960·520	4752·553	339·8
1969	164	1003·444	2368·111	332·2
TOTALS	1554	6837·855	13,154·398	

Note: columns II and III are in £m. and column IV is an index, 1956 = 100

than indicated by table 1.1. It must also be remembered however, in making such time series comparisons that inflation (both in terms of assets including revaluations and share prices) will explain some of the rise in the book value and market value indices. In column IV is the EXTEL Security Value Index obtained by taking the average of the monthly mean value over each twelve month period. While the market went up by a factor of over 3 during the period, the market value of the takeovers increased by a factor of over 40 up to 1968 and a factor of over 20 up to 1969.

A visual indication of the frequency of takeovers over the period is presented in charts 1.1a through 1.1d which indicate respectively the monthly number, book value, market value and EXTEL index. The first three have been smoothed by seasonal adjustment to ease interpretation but the monthly raw data for all series appears in appendix II.

A number of points of interest emerge from the data on the frequency of takeovers. All indices indicate a general increase in the takeover activity both in terms of number and value. However because of the sources of bias mentioned in the previous paragraph, chart 1.1a, the monthly number of takeovers gives a more representative picture of the nature of the increase through the period. From the middle of 1958 to the middle of 1959 there was a rapid increase in the number of takeovers, it doubling from roughly 5–6 per month to 11–12 per month. From then until the middle of 1963 there is a slight downward trend in activity, although it continues to exceed the pre-1958 levels. A second minor peak occurs in 1964 where the average increases from roughly just over 7 per month to around 10 per month. This level drops back to around 7 per month in the middle of 1966. From then there was a rapid increase, reaching its peak in the last half of 1968. On the smoothed data it reached a rate of over 22 takeovers per month or on average over one successful offer every business day. On the raw data, July 1968 was the month of highest activity with 28 offers being made while in December 1968 there were 27. From then until the end of the period, the activity fell off, though still exceeding the pre-1966 level at roughly 13 per month. The indications are that the takeover activity in 1970 has been maintained on an average of roughly 11–12 per month.

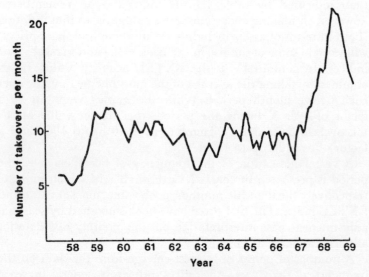

FIGURE 1.1a Monthly seasonally adjusted frequency of takeovers.

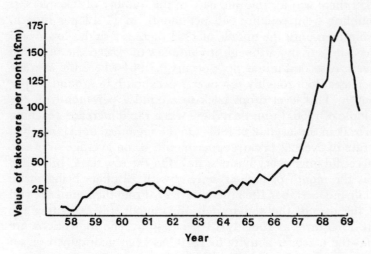

FIGURE 1.1b Monthly seasonally adjusted book value of takeovers.

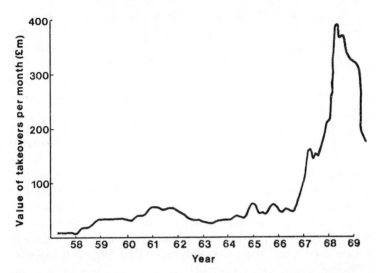

FIGURE 1.1c Monthly seasonally adjusted market value of takeovers.

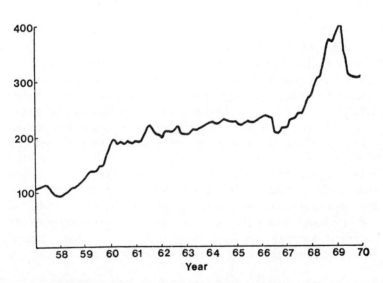

FIGURE 1.1d Extel security value index (1956 = 100).

This most recent boom within the boom emerges as the most prominent feature of the results presented. On charts 1.1b and 1.1c, it can be seen as virtually the only feature in an upward trending series. No doubt the non-emergence of the two previous minor waves of activity is due to the upward trend in the value indices due to inflation in book values and stock prices over the period.

On this point, chart 1.1d is the monthly EXTEL security value index and at first glance appears to be highly correlated with all indices of frequency. Thus, not only does the rise in stock prices account for some of the increase in the market value of takeovers, but also it raises the question of a possible causal relationship between the two. That is, the market value index and particularly the 1966–8 boom will to some extent be the result of the apparent corresponding rise in equity values in that the rise in security prices will mean that 'larger' companies are being taken over. Nevertheless, as pointed out earlier, this only accounts for a small proportion of the increase in the market value of the takeovers assuming all firms' share prices rise with the market. Further, simply the rise in the market value of firms would not account for the increase in the number of takeovers observed in chart 1.1a. Research undertaken in the U.S. by R. L. Nelson (1959 and 1966) also indicates an observable correlation between the frequency of takeovers and the index of stock prices and the business cycle, but so far a caussal explanation remains elusive.* The question of why when market prices are generally rising (or high) the takeover rate should be rising (or high) may be explained by the leaders taking over the laggers. That is, the assumption that all firms' share prices increase in a rising market may obscure the differentials or variance in stock prices that could be exaggerated in a rising market. If differentials did increase, it is clear that takeover activity is likely to increase. Acquiring firms or raiders would wish to take over other firms when their own share prices are high and when the market is optimistic since it would, on the one hand, lower the effective cost of the acquisition to the extent it was paid for by a share issue and, on the other, it would be likely the rising market would be prepared to accept

---

* For a critical view of this work see Hindley (1972).

the additional equity. Furthermore, the acquired firms, if, they are laggers, would not only be relatively 'cheap', but also would be in a weak defensive position in that for some reason or other they have failed to keep up with the market trend.

It is not possible to test this hypothesis directly with the data so far presented but the market valuation of the acquired firm is suggested for analysis in the theoretical model developed in chapter 2.

As stated earlier, over 43 per cent of the firms existing during all or part of the period 1957–69 were taken over. Table 1.1a offers a more detailed view of the survival pattern of the firms during this period. Here, the number of firms existing in each year up to 1966 is given along with the probability that they survive until 1969. This table finishes at 1966 because that year is the last in which newly quoted companies were allowed to enter the population under investigation. It can be seen that the companies existing in 1957 had only slightly better than an even chance of surviving up to 1969, while of those existing in 1966, over one-fifth were taken over during the next three years. This offers a further indication of the enormous magnitude and impact of takeovers on the pattern of industrial ownership and on the continuity of the firm as an entity over this relatively short period of time.

TABLE 1.1a

Probability of Survival – 1957–69

Year	No. of firms existing	No. taken over	Proportion surviving to 1969
1957	2487	1214	0·512
1958	2452	1149	0·531
1959	2432	1059	0·565
1960	2435	993	0·592
1961	2441	919	0·624
1962	2438	854	0·650
1963	2437	779	0·680
1964	2479	696	0·719
1965	2564	637	0·752
1966	2507	549	0·781

1.3   INDUSTRIAL PATTERN OF TAKEOVER ACTIVITY

Just as the incidence of takeovers has not been uniform over time so also has it varied between industries. It is obvious that there are significant differences between industries in terms of risk, rate of return, structure, growth in demand, 'optimal' firm size, etc. It is also likely that such differences could result in differences in the level and timing of takeover activity. Thus while discrepancies between firm's market valuation may partially explain why takeovers occur, additional motives for takeover are likely to be discovered through an examination of the industrial environment and the differences in the takeover rate which emerge.

To accomplish this, the 3566 firms in the population were allocated to 67 industrial groups, each firm being allowed to appear in one or more industries according their degree of diversification.* The distribution of firms by number of industrial classes appears in appendix I, table IV. Using these industry classifications, table 1.2 gives the ranked proportion of takeovers by industry. The most striking feature of these results is the marked differences in the takeover rate between industries. Seven industries lost over 50 per cent of their members through takeovers while 9 industries lost under 30 per cent. Also, by simply subtracting column II from column I and comparing this with column I, one can gain an indication of the effect the takeovers have had on the structure of the industry. For instance, of the 51 soft drink manufacturers which existed during the period, only 20 remain independent at its end.

A detailed discussion of the industry differences and their effect on the character of the intra-industry takeover activity will appear in chapters 3 and 4 where two models of takeovers will be tested at the industry level. I shall attempt to discover not only whether the characteristics of the firm are an important determinant of the probability of takeover but also if this applies to the characteristics of the industry. Particularly, one might expect the structure of the industry and the degree of concentration to affect the takeover rate. That is, if an industry is highly concentrated at the beginning of the period, the takeover

---

* Table V, appendix I gives the full description of the industry classes while an abbreviated description appears in table 1.2 below.

TABLE 1.2

Ranked Industry Classes by Proportion of Takeovers

Rank	Industry	I No. of companies	II No. of takeovers	III Proportion of takeovers (%)
1	Soft Drinks	51	31	60·78
2	Breweries and Distilleries	166	98	59·04
3	Chemists	74	43	58·11
4	Food	255	139	54·51
5	Textiles – Hosiery and Underwear	92	49	53·26
6	Medical Equipment	49	25	51·02
7	Textiles – Cotton	108	55	50·93
8	Stores – Tailors etc.	90	44	48·89
9	Textiles – General and Distributors	218	104	47·71
10	China, Glass and Pottery	60	28	46·67
11	Hotels and Restaurants	88	41	46·59
12	Rubber Products	50	23	46·00
13	Paints	81	37	45·68
14	Wharves and Warehouses	44	20	45·45
15	Cable Manufacturers, Rope, etc.	86	39	45·35
16	Clothing Manufacturers and Merchants	178	79	44·38
17	Animal Feeding Stuffs	70	31	44·29
18	Stores – Department and Mail Order	77	34	44·16
19	Motor Car and Cycle Manufacturers	41	18	43·90
20	Asbestos, Asphalte and Tar	46	20	43·48
21	Oil – Production, Refining and Distilling	37	16	43·24
22	Car and Cycle Accessories and Components	219	94	42·92
23	Stores – General Merchants	89	38	42·70
24	Entertainments	73	31	42·47
25	Refrigeration	33	14	42·42
26	Containers and Package Material	105	44	41·90
27	Machine Tools	245	102	41·63
28	Launderies	34	14	41·18
29	Textiles – Artificial Fabrics	134	55	41·04
30	Timber and Woodcutters	101	41	40·59
31	Aircraft Accessories and Components	116	47	40·52

TABLE 1.2 (cont.)

Rank	Industry	I No. of companies	II No. of takeovers	III Proportion of takeovers (%)
32	Textiles – Wool	129	52	40·31
33	Engineers – Electrical	282	113	40·07
34	Radio and TV, Photography	125	50	40·00
35	Miscellaneous Machinery	306	122	39·87
36	Bus and Road Haulage	43	17	39·53
37	Printers and Publishers	147	58	39·46
38	Builder's Merchants	228	88	38·60
39	Shipbuilders and Docks	45	17	37·78
40	Property	256	96	37·50
41	Newspapers	43	16	37·21
42	Leather Goods	49	18	36·73
43	Engineers – Heating and Light	188	69	36·70
44	Paper and Pulp	80	29	36·25
45	Bricks, Cement and Tiles	130	47	36·15
46	Agricultural Machinery	83	30	36·14
47	Finance and Mortgage	83	30	36·14
48	Engineers – Metal Manufacturers	250	88	35·20
49	Engineers – Marine and Mining	144	50	34·72
50	Carpets and Floor Coverings	79	27	34·18
51	Chemicals	106	36	33·96
52	Plastics	137	46	33·58
53	Tobacco and Matches	24	8	33·33
54	Shipping	71	23	32·39
55	Furnishers – Manufacturers and Stores	115	37	32·17
56	Hardware and Ironmongery	143	46	32·17
57	Ironfounders and Steel Manufacturers	135	42	31·11
58	Toys and Sporting Goods	42	13	30·95
59	Boots and Shoes	64	19	29·69
60	Office Equipment	56	16	28·57
61	Car and Cycle Dealers and Repairers	128	36	28·13
62	Engineers – Civil and Construction	187	50	26·74
63	Engineers – General	326	87	26·69
64	Stores – Jewellers	38	10	26·32
65	Engineers – Textile Machinery	34	8	23·53
66	Builders and Contractors	178	40	22·47
67	Insurance Brokers	18	3	16·67

rate is likely to be lower than for a less concentrated industry. Also, the state of demand is likely to affect the takeover rate. In declining demand conditions, one would expect a contraction of output by a reduction in the number of firms. Takeovers in such conditions can provide an alternative to the bankruptcy courts* as the means of contracting the industry's output. Additionally, if firms expect and desire growth, one would anticipate a similar though perhaps less marked result to occur under conditions of static or slowly growing demand. However, one would also expect the influence of demand to have its effect felt on the performance of the firms in the industry; falling demand tending to lower the rate of return. One could therefore argue that this would emerge from the characteristics of the firm analysis in chapters 3 and 4, rendering industry analysis trivial. In fact such reasoning is incorrect. A poorly performing firm in a growth industry could not be considered identical to an equally poorly performing firm in a contracting industry. For instance, straight comparisons between firms involved in Stores–Tailors etc. whose members had an average before tax profit rate of 16·8 per cent and an average annual growth rate of 8·9 per cent, and Insurance Brokers which on average had profits before tax of 47·8 per cent and grew at 97 per cent per year, would overlook such differences and consequently prejudice any conclusions about the nature of the takeover activity.†

In addition to the large variation in mean and median performance of firms between industries, a further indication of the importance of an examination of takeovers at the industry level is offered in table 1.3. This table contains the annual number and proportion to total of takeovers for five major industrial headings which experienced particularly heavy takeover activity: Food, Breweries and Distilleries, Engineering, Textiles

* Dewey (1961) p. 257, has taken this point further. He argues that most mergers in the US 'have virtually nothing to do with either the creation of market power or the realisation of scale economies. They are merely a civilised alternative to bankruptcy or the voluntary liquidation that transfers assets from falling to rising firms.' I shall return to this point in chapter 2.

† Appendix II, table II gives the mean and median values of industry performance for the various financial and stock market indicators.

and Building.* The takeovers in these broad industry classes accounted for nearly two thirds of all takeovers in the period.

Striking differences emerge between these industries with respect ot the timing of the waves of takeovers. In both the Breweries and Distilleries and Food industries the highest proportion of raids occurred during the 1958–60 minor takeover boom, whereas with the others the highest proportions occurred during the more recent boom, the 1958–60 wave hardly being apparent at all. Furthermore, the Engineering industry showed remarkable stability in takeover activity up to the most recent takeover boom while others display considerable variation over the same period. The general impression these results offer is that the takeover activity is to some extent an industry phenomenon. Certainly the two boom periods described earlier emerge, but it is also clear that it would not be totally correct to ascribe this solely to general valuation discrepancies resulting from a rising market index. Within the

TABLE 1.3

Annual Distribution of Takeovers in Five Major Industries

Year	Breweries	%	Food	%	Engineering	%	Textiles	%	Building	%
1957	5	5·1	5	3·6	23	5·5	12	5·4	8	5·6
1958	2	2·0	11	7·9	23	5·5	12	5·4	4	2·8
1959	15	15·3	22	15·8	25	6·0	15	6·8	4	2·8
1960	16	16·3	11	7·9	28	6·7	13	5·9	3	2·1
1961	14	14·3	9	6·5	24	5·8	7	3·2	9	6·4
1962	9	9·2	9	6·5	14	3·3	17	7·7	8	5·6
1963	6	6·1	7	5·0	21	5·0	15	6·8	8	5·6
1964	3	3·1	14	10·1	22	5·3	29	13·1	14	9·9
1965	5	5·1	14	10·1	29	7·0	11	5·0	8	5·6
1966	4	4·1	4	2·9	26	6·2	13	5·9	6	4·2
1967	9	9·2	6	4·3	48	11·5	21	9·5	13	9·2
1968	8	8·2	17	12·2	86	20·6	38	17·2	36	25·5
1969	2	2·0	10	7·2	48	11·5	18	8·1	20	14·2
TOTAL	98	100·0	139	100·0	417	†99·9	221	100·0	141	†99·9

* These last three represent combined industries – i.e. Engineering, nos. 8–17; Textiles, 38, 53–7; Building, 4–6. (See appendix I, table V).

† The discrepancy from 100·0% is due to rounding.

booms were waves of activity affecting particular industries more strongly than others. A more detailed investigation into particular industries than is possible here would no doubt throw up structural and institutional factors to which the waves could be attributed. For example, the Textile Reorganisation Commission set up in the early sixties to encourage restructuring of the textile industry and the introduction and acceptance of canister beer which can be safely transported resulting in the possibility for cost savings through large scale centralised breweries.

Thus, in formulating the model of takeovers in chapter 2, I shall test the various hypotheses concerning the acquired firms' characteristics, industry by industry. The desirability of this is indicated by the results presented in this section: industries differ in the level of takeover activity, the growth rate and the rate of return, as well as the takeover pattern over time.

1.4   CHARACTERISTICS OF RAIDERS

While the primary purpose of this study is to identify the differences between firms which are taken over and those which are not, I shall also focus attention upon the differences between raiders – firms which undertake takeovers – and the surviving firms which generally do not. The purpose of this section is to describe some of the characteristics of raiders as a means of setting the scene for the analysis of raiders' motivations in chapter 6.

Of the 1554 takeovers of firms within the population, 1244 were undertaken by raiders also within the population, the remaining 310 raids being instituted by firms outside. Table VII in appendix I gives the breakdown of these firms by the reason they were not included and the number of takeovers by the firms in each category. One can note that by far the largest category of outside raiders were non-quoted companies. The remaining 1244 takeovers were undertaken by a total of 643 raiders. Table 1.4 gives the distribution of these internal raiders by number and proportion of raids and the number and proportion of these raiders which were subsequently taken over in each category.

The first point to notice in table 1.4 is that raiding is by no means limited to a small number of select firms, for over 18 per

TABLE 1.4

Distribution of Raiders by Number of Raids

Number of raids	Number of raiders	Proportion of raiders to total (%)	Number of raiders taken over	Proportion of raiders taken over (%)
1	405	62·9	121	18·8
2	121	18·8	23	3·6
3	44	6·8	8	1·2
4	28	4·3	1	0·2
5	14	2·2	4	0·6
6	14	2·2	2	0·3
7	3	0·5	0	0·0
8	6	0·9	0	0·0
9	2	0·3	0	0·0
10	1	0·2	0	0·0
12	1	0·2	0	0·0
15	3	0·5	1	0·2
44	1	0·2	0	0·0
TOTAL	643	100·0%	160	24·9%

cent of all firms in the population undertook at least one raid. Also, it appears that raiders are to some extent partially immune from the threat of takeover as only 24·9 per cent of raiders eventually get taken over compared with 43·4 per cent of all firms. Furthermore, if a raider makes at least 2 takeovers, the proportion declines to 16·4 per cent. It further declines to 13·7 per cent and just under 11 per cent of the raiders being taken over if they make at least 3 and at least 4 raids, respectively. The most prominent raider is Courtaulds Ltd with 44 raids (mainly of small textile companies), followed by a large gap; then Slater Walker Securities Ltd, Viyella International Ltd and Whitbread Ltd each with 15 raids.

I next attempted to examine whether there were significant differences *between* the firms which made 3 or more raids in terms of various financial characteristics of the firms. Two sets of regressions were run using first, the number, and second, the value of the raids on the pre-tax profit rate,* growth rate, retention ratio, liquidity ratio, valuation ratio, and average size.† A sample of these results appears in table 1.5 below. Taking the level of significance of the estimated coefficient of 5 per cent or approximately twice its standard error, it can readily be seen that in no case is any of the variables a significant determinant of either the number or value of the takeovers made by an individual raider. This would tend to indicate that the body

TABLE 1.5

Raiders Regression Results

	Constant	Profit Rate	Growth Rate	Retn Ratio
1	4·7364 (1·1620)	−2·2813 (2·5970)	0·2248 (0·3242)	1·6142 (2·5713)
2	4·8289 (0·8571)			
3	55·5792 (16·7944)	−22·3027 (37·5345)	−0·9851 (4·6862)	−37·0465 (37·1633)
4	40·5179 (12·3737)			

	Liq. Ratio	Valuation Ratio	Size	R^2
1	1·9115 (2·0193)			0·016
2		−0·0696 (0·5630)	0·0050 (0·0030)	0·025
3	20·7851 (29·1860)			0·023
4		−8·7921 (8·1278)	0·0632 (0·0432)	0·034

Note: numbers in brackets are the standard errors of the associated coefficients.

Note: the dependent variable in regressions 1 and 2 is the number of takeovers while the dependant variable in 3 and 4 is the market value of the raider's acquisitions.

* Profits after tax and cash flow were also tried in place of pre-tax profits but they produced similar results and therefore are not shown.
† These independent variables are defined in appendix I, section II.G.

of raiders (i.e. the 117 firms which had undertaken 3 or more raids during the period)is extremely homogeneous. Firms which undertook the largest number (or value) of raids were neither more nor less profitable than firms undertaking the smaller number (or value); nor did they grow faster or retain more or less, nor were they more or less liquid, valued higher or lower on the market or of significantly different size. These conclusions will be of relevance when I come to examine raiders' performance with respect to the performance of firms in their respective industries in chapter 6, for it lends support to the methodology adopted of treating raiders and their motivations as a reasonably homogeneous group.

Up to now in the discussion of the motivations behind takeovers I have tacitly assumed that takeovers occurred primarily within the same industry boundaries. To examine whether or not this tends to be the case I took a sample of 593 takeovers which represented the total takeovers undertaken by the 117 firms which had made 3 or more raids. These were classified as horizontal (the same stage of the industrial process), or vertical (either a supplier or distributor of the raiders primary output) or conglomerate (where no apparent productive links exist). The result of this is that 438 of the sub-sample of raids or just under 74 per cent were horizontal, 108 or just over 18 per cent were vertical and only 47, or less than 8 per cent could be classified as conglomerate. (It may be of interest to note that all but 10 of the conglomerate takeovers occurred between 1965 and 1969). Thus, while conglomerates and their importance appear to be increasing, they as yet have marginal bearing on the UK takeover scene and hence do not command that degree of interest which they have merited in the US. For the rest, takeovers by the 117 raiders are primarily within the same industrial activity or at a different stage of related industrial processes.

To shed further light on this and to see whether the presence of a large number of raiders in an industry tends to result in greater takeover activity than if few were present, I again used the 117 raiders which had undertaken 3 or more takeovers and ranked the 67 industries by the number of raiders in each.*

* Because of the procedure of multiple industry classes adopted, the 117 raiders usually appear in more than one industry.

I also ranked the industries by number of raids and proportion of raids* and calculated rank correlation coefficients and significance tests. The results of this are as follows:

Number of raiders with proportion of takeovers

$r = 0.299$ $z = 2.428$ which is significant at the 5 per cent level

Number of raiders with number of takeovers

$r = 0.789$ $z = 6.407$ which is significant at the 1 per cent level

Thus is would appear that the presence of raiders in an industry is associated with the takeover activity in that industry; in other words most of the takeover activity is horizontal in nature. This apparent restatement of the earlier results is included lest queries arise over the method of classifying takeovers as horizontal, vertical or conglomerate. Moreover, these latter results are for the number and proportion of all takeovers in each industry and thus confirm the pattern which was apparent from the sub-sample of 593 takeovers previously employed.

The purpose of presenting the results and discussion included in this section is to set the scene for an analysis of the characteristics of raiders and their implications to the theory of the firm in chapter 6. The latter results relating raiders to industry classes will also have bearing on the industry analysis undertaken in chapter 3 and 4.

1.5 PERFORMANCE OF TAKEN OVER FIRMS CONTRASTED WITH NON-TAKEN OVER FIRMS

In this section I shall present some very crude results, the purpose of which is suggestive for the more detailed analysis of the differences between taken over and non-taken over firms in chapters 3 and 4. In table 1.6 are the mean values over the entire time period of six characteristics of the firm for the two groups – taken over firms and non-taken over firms – and the percentages that the characteristics of the taken over firms are of the non-taken over firms. As can easily be seen for the profit rate, growth rate, valuation ratio and size, there are large

* See appendix II, table III for the data.

differences between the two groups) the growth rate of taken over firms being approximately 60 per cent of the value for the surviving firms. The retention ratio and liquidity ratio offer less important inter-group differences, each being greater than 80 per cent of the surviving group's mean. Thus, for the three most important indices of performance — profits, growth and valuation – the acquired firms performed substantially worse than firms which survived.

TABLE 1.6

Mean Values of Performance of Acquired and Surviving Firms

Variable	Mean value of takeover	Mean value of non-takeover	% of column 1 to 2
Pre-tax profit rate	0·1151	0·1932	59·6
Growth rate	0·0760	0·1905	39·9
Retention ratio	0·3365	0·4064	82·8
Liquidity ratio	−0·0580	−0·0700	82·9
Valuation ratio	0·8627	1·5214	56·7
Size (net assets) £m.	4·9974	8·0097	62·4

The crude data in the above table gives, however, no indication of the variance or overlap between the two groups. Furthermore, while there are large differences between the means for some variables, the skewness of the distribution could be serving to make the groups appear to be more distinct than they really are. For example, if few of the very largest firms are taken over, the mean value presented in the above table could overstate the actual group separation, based on the full distribution. In table 1.7 are the median values of the same six variables, which offers a better indication of central tendency than the mean for skewed distributions. Indeed, by examining the median values one finds that not only does the effect of the retention ratio and liquidity ratio virtually disappear, but so does that of size. Profits, growth and valuation, however, only marginally change; in fact the difference being accentuated with respect to the growth rate.

TABLE 1.7

Median Values of Performance of Acquired and Surviving Firms

Variable	Median value of takeover	Median value of non-takeover	% of column 1 to 2
Pre-tax profit rate	0·0855	0·1276	67·0
Growth rate	0·0228	0·0982	23·3
Retention ratio	0·3360	0·3300	101·8
Liquidity ratio	−0·1571	−0·1741	90·2
Valuation ratio	0·6295	0·9780	64·4
Size (net assets) £m.	1·4491	1·5697	92·3

Neither table 1.6 nor 1.7 shed light on the problem of within-group variation or overlap between the two groups with respect to the indices. Although the differences in means or medians gives some indication that the performance of the two groups is likely to be different, it does not tell us either the degree of overlap nor does it give any indication of the extent of any systematic relationship operating such that a change in the performance of one firm would increase the likelihood that it gets taken over. I shall leave discussion of the latter point to chapter 5 where the probit model of takeovers will be developed. Meanwhile, the following data in tables 1.8a to 1.8e offers a visual indication of the overlap of the two groups. In each table is grouped data by variable of the number of acquired and surviving firms and the proportion of taken over firms to the total in each group. Liquidity is omitted for this analysis because no relationship emerges.

All variables show a large degree of overlap, none providing a perfect discriminator between the two groups of acquired and surviving firms. If, however, instead of thinking in terms of separating the two groups on the basis of performance variables such that one is attempting to find critical values of the variables beyond which the firm will certainly get taken over, one considers the movement of the variables in terms of increasing or decreasing the probability of being taken over, then the data presented below takes on considerable significance. All variables except size and retentions, which seems

TABLE 1.8a

Numbers of Surviving and Acquired Firms for Grouped Pre-tax Profit Rate*

Group		No. of surviving firms	No. of acquired firms	Proportion to total in group
−0·50 −	−0·10	2	34	0·944
−0·10 −	0·00	19	81	0·810
0·00 −	0·05	91	163	0·642
0·05 −	0·10	308	347	0·530
0·10 −	0·13	249	214	0·521
0·13 −	0·17	367	234	0·389
0·17 −	0·20	234	129	0·355
0·20 −	0·25	287	148	0·340
0·25 −	0·30	168	90	0·349
0·30 −	0·40	160	70	0·304
0·40 −	0·50	66	22	0·250
0·50 −	1·00	53	19	0·264
1·00 −	over	8	3	0·375
TOTAL		2012	1554	

* Profits after tax and cash flow were also grouped and results similar to those of pre-tax profits were obtained.

TABLE 1.8b

Numbers of Surviving and Acquired Firms for Grouped Growth Rate

Group		No. of surviving firms	No. of acquired firms	Proportion to total in group
−0·50 −	−0·10	2	40	0·952
−0·10 −	0·00	93	268	0·742
0·00 −	0·03	143	305	0·681
0·03 −	0·07	276	346	0·556
0·07 −	0·10	219	150	0·407
0·10 −	0·15	291	156	0·349
0·15 −	0·20	224	83	0·270
0·20 −	0·30	268	89	0·249
0·30 −	0·40	143	42	0·227
0·40 −	0·50	70	23	0·247
0·50 −	0·70	98	28	0·222
0·70 −	1·00	53	13	0·197
1·00 −	over	132	11	0·077
TOTAL		2012	1554	

TABLE 1.8c
Numbers of Surviving and Acquired Firms for Grouped Retention Ratio

Group	No. of surviving firms	No. of acquired firms	Proportion to total in group
−9·99 − −1·00	11	17	0·607
−1·00 − −0·50	13	22	0·629
−0·50 − −0·20	20	32	0·615
−0·20 − −0·10	7	23	0·767
−0·10 − 0·00	20	43	0·683
0·00 − 0·10	70	76	0·521
0·10 − 0·20	113	117	0·509
0·20 − 0·30	175	144	0·451
0·30 − 0·40	358	219	0·380
0·40 − 0·50	486	233	0·324
0·50 − 0·60	388	242	0·384
0·60 − 0·70	191	138	0·419
0·70 − 0·80	79	59	0·428
0·80 − 0·90	24	23	0·489
0·90 − 1·00	20	62	0·756
1·00 − over	37	104	0·737
TOTAL	2012	1554	

TABLE 1.8d
Numbers of Surviving and Acquired Firms for Grouped Valuation Ratio

Group	No. of surviving firms	No. of acquired firms	Proportion to total in group
0·00 − 0·20	3	37	0·925
0·20 − 0·30	9	89	0·908
0·30 − 0·40	19	116	0·859
0·40 − 0·50	48	172	0·782
0·50 − 0·60	77	187	0·708
0·60 − 0·70	100	135	0·574
0·70 − 0·80	140	139	0·498
0·80 − 0·90	136	116	0·460
0·90 − 1·10	287	160	0·358
1·10 − 1·30	240	133	0·357
1·30 − 1·50	201	76	0·274
1·50 − 1·70	161	51	0·241
1·70 − 2·00	181	50	0·216
2·00 − 3·00	240	66	0·216
3·00 − 4·00	72	7	0·089
4·00 − over	98	20	0·169
TOTAL	2012	1554	

TABLE 1·8e

Numbers of Surviving and Acquired Firms for Grouped Size

£m. Group	No. of surviving firms	No. of acquired firms	Proportion to total in group
0 – 1	787	627	0·443
1 – 2	385	334	0·465
2 – 4	349	250	0·417
4 – 7	178	140	0·440
7 – 10	76	64	0·457
10 – 15	72	47	0·395
15 – 20	44	29	0·399
20 – 30	40	33	0·452
30 – 125	61	27	0·307
125 – 500	16	3	0·158
500 – over	4	0	0·000

to possess a U-shaped distribution,* appear to move virtually monotonically from one extreme to the other and thus, with the above interpretation, can be used to describe the way in which the level of any given variable for a firm will determine its probability of being taken over and also how a firm can alter the probability by changing its financial policies. The theoretical underpinnings behind each variable's effect on the likelihood of takeover will be considered in the next chapter and the data contained in tables 1.8a through 1.8e will be statistically analysed in the probit model in chapter 5.

Possibly the most important reason for choosing the above modification to the critical level interpretation is that of omitted variables. With any cross-section study there will be random variation in such a critical level as well as variation attributable to omitted or unspecificable variables. The most important omitted variable is likely to be the industry climate as indicated by the data presented in section 1.3 above. Thus one could interpret the data presented in the previous tables as encompassing a distribution of individual firm's critical levels

---

* I shall return to this point in chapter 4.

for the various variables, they (the critical levels) differing not only as the result of random variation, but also because of various aspects of their industrial settings. I shall return to this interpretation in chapter 5 as it forms the basis of the probit model of takeovers.

A less important but yet interesting aspect of the difference between taken over and surviving firms is the age distribution of the two groups. Since firms entering the population of public quoted companies were included up to June 1966, the youngest a firm could be as of December 1970* would be 4½ years old. Table 1.9 gives the age distribution of taken over firms and surviving firms as measured by the difference between the date at which the firm went public and the base date of December 1970 and the proportion of firms taken over in each age group.

As indicated by the proportions, there appears to be a greater incidence of takeovers of older companies than of young ones. Of the 1768 firms which went public since the last war, only 582, or less than one-third have been taken over while of the 1798 firms which went public during or before the war,

TABLE 1.9

Age Distribution of Taken over and Surviving Firms

Age group (years)	No. of survivors	No. of takeovers	Proportion to total in group
4½ – 10	465	120	20·5
10 – 15	178	105	37·1
15 – 20	184	136	42·5
20 – 25	259	221	46·0
25 – 30	16	16	50·0
30 – 35	170	168	49·7
35 – 40	93	110	54·2
40 – 45	145	149	50·7
45 – 50	77	88	53·3
50 – 60	70	70	50·0
60 – over	355	371	51·1
TOTAL	2012	1554	

* See appendix I sections I.3 and J.3 for a description of this age variable.

972, or well over one-half, were taken over. There are likely to be several reasons for this. First, the low incidence of takeover in the youngest firms is probably due to the fact that normally, at least for the first few years after going public, control (i.e. over 50 per cent of the voting power) is retained in the hands of the directors making an involuntary takeover impossible Second, one would think that the managerial motivations (e.g. growth) which prompted the firm to go public in the first place would set it apart from the performance of the typical taken over firm which, as we have already seen in this section, tends to be poor.*

1.6 THE METHOD OF PAYMENT AND THE BID PREMIUM

In this section I shall describe two further aspects of the takeover scene – the method used for payment for the acquired firm and the premium over the pre-offer price that the acquiring firm has paid.

Payment practices employed in the takeover process have been categorised into five basic groups; cash only, cash plus some of the raider's shares, shares only, convertible unsecured loan stock or loan stock plus shares, and finally by a company exchange whereby the terms agreed are that the company to be acquired agrees to purchase a subsidiary of the raider, paying for it by the issue of a sufficient number of its shares to give the raider voting control.† Table 1.10 gives the distribution of the various payment practices and the way each has varied over time. As the figures represent the terms of the successful offers, they conceal a cash component present in virtually all take-overs – that cash used to acquire shares through the market prior to or during negotiations. From table 1.10 it can be seen that the most common method of payment was a cash offer for

---

* A similar argument is put forward by Ma (1960). He suggests that higher mortality rates of older companies (both bankruptcy and takeover) may be due to their failure to supply dynamic management, the tendency to be conservative, the fact that young companies are still experiencing the phase of expansion which brought them into the market, the possibility that entry requirements have been made more stringent over time and, finally, the decline in concentration of certain old industries.

† See appendix I, Section II J.4 for a more complete description of the offer terms.

TABLE 1.10

Method of Payment over Time

Year	Cash	%	Cash & share	%	Share	%	Loan stock	%	Company exchange %		Year Total	%
1957	31	40·8	12	15·8	31	40·8	1	1·3	1	1·3	76	100·0
1958	44	53·0	15	18·1	22	26·5	1	1·2	1	1·2	83	100·0
1959	75	54·3	29	21·0	33	23·9	0	0·0	1	0·7	138	99·9*
1960	47	43·9	21	19·6	38	35·5	1	0·9	0	0·0	107	99·9*
1961	38	33·6	36	31·9	36	31·9	3	2·7	0	0·0	113	100·1*
1962	40	40·8	17	17·3	35	35·7	4	4·1	2	2·0	98	99·9*
1963	41	45·6	21	23·3	19	21·1	6	6·7	3	3·3	90	100·0
1964	57	50·9	24	21·4	26	23·2	2	1·8	3	2·7	112	100·0
1965	43	43·0	26	26·0	21	21·0	7	7·0	3	3·0	100	100·0
1966	23	25·8	25	28·1	19	21·3	22	24·7	0	0·0	89	99·9*
1967	57	39·6	36	25·0	15	10·4	33	22·9	3	2·1	144	100·0
1968	70	29·2	43	17·9	53	22·2	72	30·0	2	0·8	240	100·1*
1969	44	26·8	31	18·9	42	25·6	47	28·6	0	0·0	164	99·9*
	610		336		390		199		19		1554	Totals

* Deviations from 100·0% are due to rounding errors.

the shares of the acquired firm. This method was used in just under 40 per cent of the cases. A share exchange was the second most common form of offer and was used in just under 25 per cent of the takeovers. The third most frequent payment practice was a combination of the first two, whereby the offer involved a share exchange with an additional cash inducement. This was used in just under 21 per cent of the takeovers. The employment of convertible unsecured loan stock by itself or in combination with some of the raiders' shares was used in over 12 per cent of the takeovers and finally there were 19 cases where a company exchange formed the basis of the acquisition. The most prominent point to notice in the lower part of table 1.10 is that in the most recent takeover boom, convertible unsecured loan stock was frequently chosen as the method of payment, while previously it was virtually unknown. The advantage of this as a form of payment is that it neither affects one's liquidity position as would a cash payment nor does it dilute one's equity if the company is acquired at a price in excess of its book value. Furthermore, it appears to have been perhaps more readily acceptable to the owners and the market than would a total payment of shares. It does, however, result in the raider becoming more highly geared but this may not be particularly worrying if he can earn more than the usual 7–8 per cent required to service the loan stock on the acquired assets. On top of this, the issue of convertibles for takeovers provide a handy way to alter the capital structure of a firm which desires growth but whose past record prevents it from seeking funds directly through the capital market. The use of loan stock appears to have caused some reduction in the percentage of the other three main methods of payment although the chief method to suffer was that of cash offer. This is not surprising as the recent takeover boom occurred during an optimistic rising stock market and a period of government financial controls on bank lending. In the 1959–60 minor takeover boom, however, there appears to be no corresponding fall in the use of cash for acquisitions, it continuing to account for over one-half of the takeovers in 1958 and 1959.

While considering payments practices as an aspect of the takeover scene, I also attempted to examine the determination of the bid premium, i.e. the amount the raider pays in excess of the pre-bid price of the shares of the firm(s) it acquires. This was measured by the difference between the lowest share price that operated in the year of the offer (or in the previous year if the offer occurred too early in the year for a representative pre-bid price to have been established free of any offer reaction) and the final offer price per share, normalised by dividing by the low share price in order to arrive at the percentage increase in the share price. A sub-sample of the total takeovers is employed in the analysis of the bid premium comprising 593 offers undertaken by the 117 raiders previously examined in section 1.4 above. Such a stratified sample was used to simplify the process of relating the bid premium to raider's characteristics as well as those of the acquired firm.

The primary hypothesis I wished to examine is that the bid premium will depend on the relative financial strengths of the raider and the acquired firm. The terms offered and subsequent negotiations will depend on the raider's relative strength and his ability to pay, the acquired firm's ability to offer a defense and thereby improve the terms, and the market's reaction to the bid which could result in upward adjustments to both the acquired firm's and the raider's valuation. Both would affect the bid premium, the former indirectly through the possibility of an improved offer and the latter to the extent that the offer contained a component of the raider's shares.*

The model assumes that:

$$BP = BP(S_R, - S_{AF}, P_R, P_{AF}, L_R, L_{AF},) \qquad (1)$$

and

$$BP = BP(S_R - S_{AF}, VR_R, VR_{AF}, L_R, L_{AF},) \qquad (2)$$

where BP is the bid premium, S_R is the raider's size (net assets), S_{AF} is the acquired firm's size, so that $S_R - S_{AF}$ is the difference between the raider's size and the acquired firm's size and hence a measure of their relative strengths, P_R is the raider's profit rate (before tax), P_{AF} is the acquired firm's profit rate (before tax), L_R is the raider's liquidity ratio, L_{AF} is the acquired firm's liquidity ratio, VR_R is the raider's valuation ratio prior to the offer, and VR_{AF} is the acquired firm's valuation ratio prior to the offer – both being measured with the annual low share price in the numerator. All variables except the last two were measured at the latest accounting period prior to the offer.

It is anticipated that:

$$\partial BP/\partial(S_R - S_{AF}) \quad < 0 \qquad \text{(a)}$$
$$\partial BP/\partial VR_R \quad > 0 \qquad \text{(b)}$$
$$\partial BP/\partial VR_{AF} \quad < 0 \qquad \text{(c)}$$
$$\partial BP/\partial L_R \quad > 0 \qquad \text{(d)}$$
$$\partial BP/\partial L_{AF} \quad > 0 \qquad \text{(e)}$$
$$\partial BP/\partial P_R \quad > 0 \qquad \text{(f)}$$
$$\partial BP/\partial P_{AF} \quad > 0 \qquad \text{(g)}$$

The anticipated relationship in (a) asserts that the greater the size difference between the raider and the acquired firm, the

---

* Manne (1965) has suggested that by looking at the bid premium and the movements of the raider's shares upon the announcement of the offer it might be possible to distinguish between mergers motivated by monopoly profit and those trying to establish more efficient management in poorly run companies. He postulated that the former would result in an increase in both raider's and acquired firm's share prices whereas the latter would result in a decline in the price of the raider's shares. Primarily motivated by the social implications of this suggestion, he was, however, unable to test it empirically.

weaker the acquired firm's relative defensive position in terms of bargaining power* and the less chance there will be of attracting other raiders with higher bids seeking to block the original raider from increasing his market share. Both factors would tend to have a dampening effect on the bid premium. The relationship in (b) states that the higher the raider's valuation ratio the greater the bid premium and it is based on the fact that a high valuation ratio will effectively lower the cost of the acquisition to the extent that the raider's shares form part or all of the offer so that the raider could afford to 'pay' more for the acquired firm's assets. Relationship (c) states that the lower the acquired firm's valuation ratio, the weaker its defensive position, the lower market valuation most likely being the result of a poor profit record and poor future expectations. Despite the acquired firm's argument that it may be an artificially low valuation, it is the market which sets the valuation and it is up to the market to accept any offer terms which would improve on the pre-bid price of the acquired firm's shares. The partial relationship of (d) is a statement of the raider's ability to pay for the acquired firm out of liquid assets such that the more liquid the more it could afford to pay either in a cash offer or an offer with a cash component.† The relationship of (e) states that the acquired firm's liquidity will positively affect the bid premium and is based on the improved defensive position that ready cash would offer.‡ The relationships of (f) and (g) follow from what has already been asserted with respect to the valuation ratio. They therefore represent alternative but possibly more directly causal relationships with the bid premium than (b) and (c). It is for this reason the two sets of variables appear in separate equations.

Multiple linear regressions were undertaken on the two equations in (1) and (2) above and the results appear in table 1.11. In general these results seem to indicate that the

---

* See section 1.8 for a discussion of the defensive strategies adopted by acquired firms.

† Over 60 percent of all takeovers contained a cash component in the offer, either in total or with some other form of payment (see table 1.10 above) and in virtually all takeovers cash was used to acquire shares on the market.

‡ See section 1.8 for a discussion of the defensive strategies.

TABLE 1.11

Bid Premium Regression Results

Regression	Constant	$S_R - S_{AF}$	P_R	P_{AF}	L_R	L_{AF}	R^2
1	0·85582 (0·11885)	−0·00005 (0·00035)	0·87402 (0·21765)	−0·73507 (0·34869)	−0·09757 (0·20772)	0·16971 (0·20772)	0·05761

Regression	Constant	$S_R - S_{AF}$	VR_R	VR_{AF}	L_R	L_{AF}	R^2
2	0·85838 (0·12436)	−0·00009 (0·00035)	−0·07783 (0·07215)	0·00514 (0·05212)	−0·07041 (0·20915)	0·17962 (0·22565)	0·00185

Note: standard errors appear in brackets below the associated parameter estimates.

particular specification of the various variables likely to enter into the relationship have had no appreciable effect on the bid premium. The only two significant parameter estimates at the 5 per cent probability level are the raider's profit rate (P_R) and the acquired firm's profit rate (P_{AF}) although the latter takes on the opposite sign from that anticipated. It is difficult to see how this latter result could be interpreted especially since the parameter estimate for VR_{AF} proved to be insignificant. That is, the low profits causing a high bid premium do not appear to act through the valuation ratio as anticipated by the alternative specifications of equations (1) and (2). Aside from profitability, only the size difference variable $(S_R - S_{AF})$ and the acquired firm's liquidity ratio take on the sign anticipated from relationships (a) through (e) although none are statistically significant.

It was perhaps optimistic to expect the above models to adequately explain what is, after all, an extremely complex operation involving not only various aspects of the performance of the firms involved but also the personalities of the individuals concerned with the negotiations. It would appear that the 'noise' generated from the latter source has prevented the emergence of the anticipated relationship. Nevertheless, while the profit rate of the raider remains a significant determinant of the bid premium, on its own it explains at best less than 4 per cent of the variation in the bid premium. Unfortunately, by itself this is not particularly informative. One does not know whether the high profits are in some way promoting optimism through to the offer terms or whether it is due to a third factor such as the industrial structure – an oligopolistic structure allowing high profits for the raider but also increasing the competitiveness by other firms in the industry for the expansion of market share by acquisition, the competition for the acquired firm (either actual or potential) causing the bid premium to be raised.

1.7   TAKEOVERS AND MERGERS – DEFINITIONS AND TREATMENT

While the vast majority of the takeovers were undertaken by the usual method of one firm making a conditional offer for the shares of another, in 39 cases there occurred a merger whereby a new company was formed to acquire the assets of the two or more companies involved in the negotiations. In all cases the shares of the new company were exchanged in agreed proportions for the shares of the merging companies and therefore are not contested takeovers. Nevertheless, with the takeovers undertaken by conditional offer they may be either agreed or contested and there was no readily available means of discovering which. For this reason, rather than reject these 39 mergers which took their form usually for financial convenience rather than because they were singled out for their element of agreement, I attempted to identify the dominant firm in the negotiations in order to classify the companies as raider or acquired firm(s). In any case, to omit the companies would serve to bias the industry results undertaken in chapters 3, 4 and 6. Appendix I section II.B contains the procedure adopted to identify the firms involved in the 39 mergers. Basically one wishes to discover which company was strongest at the time of the negotiations and also therefore which merged with control of the new company. Three methods are used to accomplish this classification of companies into the categories of raider or acquired firm(s); (a) the composition of the new board of directors from the boards of the merging companies, (b) the book value of the merging firms, and (c) the market value of the merging firms. A system of weighting the various posts on the new board was used so that it was possible to identify which of the merging companies were able to place their board in the key positions in the new company. I looked at the new company two years after the merger to give a representative view of the control of the new company since token positions may be given to the directors of the weaker company in the merger negotiations which are subsequently phased out by 'golden handshake'. The other two procedures adopted were to look at the relative sizes, both book value and market value, of the merging companies as the control of the new company through the offer terms agreed will largely be determined by the relative sizes of the participants – the largest firm obtaining a greater proportion of the voting shares of the new company. I was able with the use of these procedures to satisfactorily classify the merging companies as raiders or acquired firms because of the high degree of agreement between the three procedures.

1.8 UNSUCCESSFUL TAKEOVER BIDS AND DEFENSVE STRATEGIES EMPLOYED

As noted in appendix I section J.6, it was possible to identify unsuccessful takeover bids as from January 1966. There were 44 failed offers of firms (which were not later taken over in the period up to December 1969) mentioned in the press during this four year boom period while there were 637 successful takeovers in the same period. These failures represent approximately $6\frac{1}{2}$ per cent of the total offers made. Of course, there were many more failed offers resulting not only from a battle between several firms for control of another firm, one of whom was eventually successful, but also a failed offer for a firm which was later successfully taken over in the sample period.

I have not undertaken an analysis of the performance of the firms which were able to fend off an offer as opposed to those who were unable to or those who welcomed the offer because of the small number of unsuccessful takeovers.* There are, however, indications from press reports of how these 44 companies were able to avoid being taken over. The analysis of the financial characteristics and performance of taken over and surviving firms in chapters 3 and 4 will have obvious implications on the policies a firm should adopt in order to avoid being taken over (e.g. adopt policies to raise or keep up the valuation ratio). Once an offer has been made, however, it will be up to the persuasiveness of the director's arguments on both sides of a contested bid which will either frustrate or assist the offer or, more usually, affect the terms offered by raising the market valuation of the company for which the offer has been made. Contesting a bid can also have the effect of attracting a second (or third) bidder thus tending to improve the terms or divide the opposition making success more difficult. The arguments employed by the directors of the firm under offer range from the inadequacy of the terms by explaining past performance and giving optimistic forecasts for the future to criticisms of the offering company especially when there is a share component to

---

* An attempt to do just this was made by Duvall and Austin (1965). Using discriminant analysis they found the worse the performance of a company the greater chance for success by the raider and that firms which had contests (either for partial or total control) generally performed worse in terms of rate of return than their respective industries.

the offer terms. More concrete moves can be undertaken to frustrate a bid such as raising the dividend, purchasing its own shares on the market which would both help to prevent the raider gaining control and also tend to push up the market price of its own shares, seeking assistance from merchant banks or even other firms in the industry who might wish to prevent the raider from increasing its market share, waging a takeover itself and paying by a share issue to reduce the proportion of shares the raider has acquired and to place these new shares in more friendly hands and finally inviting a more friendly bidder to offer for the shares of the firm in the hope they would offer more job security to the directors of the firm under offer.*

Simply for directors to attempt to enlist support through press propaganda has in general been unsuccessful in staving off an offer. The more positive actions mentioned in the previous paragraph have brought some limited success to the firm under offer. After all, most takeovers are contested to some degree but nevertheless, the vast majority are successful. The most usual reason for the failure of an offer is that the directors control sufficient shares or sufficient shares are in friendly hands to block any takeover attempt. It has been the case in at least 12 of the 44 unsuccessful takeovers that the directors controlled over 50 per cent of the voting equity making an unwanted takeover impossible. Others were undoubtedly blocked by directors holding a substantial minority of the equity and then enlisting support from other large shareholders to prevent the acquisition. At least another three unsuccessful offers were referred to the Monopolies Commission which subsequently blocked the proposed takeover. These two causes of failure point out a difference within the group of firms which were able to avoid being taken over. Thirty-five of the failed takeovers were small firms having net assets of less than £5m. The rest except for one with net assets of £12m. all had net assets in excess of £20m. Table 1.12 gives the grouped size distribution of these companies which were able to thwart an offer for their shares.

It is in the £5m.-and-under group of companies that at least 12 takeovers attempts were blocked because directors possessed

---

* See Hayes and Taussig (1967) for a discussion of similar strategies employed in the US.

TABLE 1.12

Size Distribution of Unsuccessful Takeover Bids

Size (£m.)	Number of companies
0 – 1	15
1 – 2	6
2 – 3	7
3 – 4	4
4 – 5	0
5 – 6	3
6 – 10	0
10 – 15	1
15 – 20	0
20 – 30	5
30 – 40	0
40 – 50	1
50 – 70	0
70 – 100	2
TOTAL	44

voting control and would not sell. The intervention by the Monopolies Commission blocking the offer occurred in the £20m.-and-above size groups. Thus it would seem from the small proportion of failed to successful takeovers and the fact that probably at least half of the unsuccessful takeover bids were prevented either by the government or through voting control being within the firm or in friendly hands, there is little a firm can do to avoid being taken over once the offer has been made.

1.9 THE ACQUIRED FIRM'S ACCOUNTING DATE AND THE
        TIMING OF THE OFFER

Using the data collected on the offer date and the date the firm's accounts close for the year, it is possible to examine whether there is any tendency for the raider to time its offer with respect to the closing of the accounts of the firm which it is attempting to takeover. Since I shall be basing much of the argument in the next four chapters on the assumption that the financial performance of the firm will affect the likelihood of its being taken over, it might be expected that the offer would be instituted with respect to the availability of the latest performance information on the firm. The accounting date, however, is not the date on which the accounts are presented to the shareholders at the annual general meeting and published in the press. This usually occurs about six months after the date on which the accounts close, although in some cases when the firm is in some sort of financial difficulty such as making a large loss and possibly reorganizing its internal structure, the lag can be as much as two years.

By plotting the distribution of the number of months between the latest accounting date for which accounts were subsequently presented and the date of the offer for the firm's shares, against the number of takeovers corresponding to each, one can discover whether there appears to be any pervasive tendency for the raiders to time their offers with respect to the availability of the latest accounting data of the firm they wish to acquire. This distribution is presented in table 1.13 below and plotted in figure 1.2.

As mentioned earlier, there is a small number of firms which were bid for which had failed to produce accounts for a long time after they had closed their books, usually because they had

TABLE 1.13

Distribution of Takeovers by Time between Accounting Year End and Offer

No. of months	No. of takeovers	No. of months	No. of takeovers	No. of months	No. of takeovers
0	2	9	142	18	9
1	11	10	139	19	5
2	31	11	146	20	1
3	58	12	119	21	1
4	90	13	82	22	0
5	115	14	93	23	1
6	107	15	55	24	0
7	143	16	32	25	1
8	141	17	28	26	2
TOTALS	698		836		20 = 1554

experienced some sort of financial difficulty during that accounting period. This explanation would roughly cover the takeovers in the third column of table 1.13 or those for which the
time between the accounting year end for the last published
accounts was 18 months or more. Where the interval is less than
18 months there does appear to be a systematic relationship
between the timing of the offer and the accounting date. The
approximate bell-shaped distribution that results when the data
is plotted shows a sharp increase in the number of offers up to
7 months after the accounting date, the level of activity being
maintained over the next 4 months and then declining there-
after. The most likely explanation for this is that given a lag of
roughly 5 to 7 months between the date on which the books
close and the publication of the results, raiders seem to be
timing the offer with respect to the time when the latest
results have been made available. Thus the mechanism would
appear to be that following the publication of the results, the
raider formulates an offer on the basis of these results and then
makes the offer formal, the formulation of the offer terms
requiring some time as well. This is consistent with the plateau

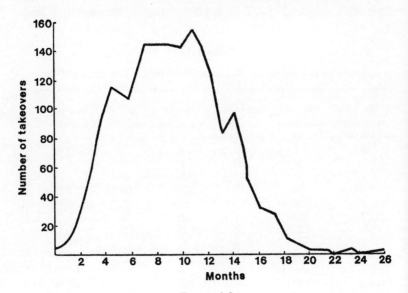

FIGURE 1.2

in the number of offers between 7 and 11 months after the accounting data.

Of course there are a number of other factors that would enter into the decision and timing of the offer, the most important being the share price of the firm which the raider is considering acquiring and the raider's own share price if he intends to pay for the firm with some of his shares. Also, firms give some indication of their performance during the year by way of interim statements and dividends and the raider could act on the basis of these. Nevertheless, from table 1.13 and the associated diagram, the indications are that the raider's decision to make an offer for the shares of another firm is based predominantly on the publication of a comprehensive account of the state of this firm and that the formal offer is made shortly after this information is made available.

The evidence and explanation offered above will be used in the next chapter where the model of takeovers is based upon the comparative financial performance of acquired and non-acquired firms. That is, the evidence is consistent with the assumption that will be employed, namely that at least part of the explanation of why firms are taken over lies with their financial performance as indicated by accounting data. And thus, it is assumed to be on such data that the raider is acting when he decides to undertake an offer for the firm's share capital.

1.10 SUMMARY

As stated in the first section of this chapter, the purpose was to describe and analyse a number of aspects of the recent takeover activity as well as set the scene for the development in the next chapter of a model of takeovers. On doing so I have accomplished the first aim of this study.

A number of hypotheses concerning the causes of takeovers have been raised in this chapter. Specifically, it was suggested that the large inter-industry differences in the takeover rate could be attributed to various industry characteristics, e.g. the state of demand, concentration, rate of return, etc. To ignore the industrial setting therefore would be to omit an essential element of the causes of takeover. Additionally, various financial and stock market variables relating to the firm including its profit rate, growth rate, retention ratio, liquidity ratio, size, and valuation ratio were suggested as influences on whether or not it was taken over. These took on relevance in addition to that offered by the individual financial variables because there was some evidence that the offer occurred in conjunction with the publication of these financial variables in the firm's annual accounts. Finally, attention was drawn to the characteristics of the raider where it emerged that the group of firms which had undertaken 3 or more raids was reasonably homogeneous. This fact will be used in chapter 6 where the characteristics of raiders will be related to the characteristics of non-raiders to indicate differences and to see what these differences might imply about the raider's motivations and the theory of the firm.

2 Stock Market
and Financial Variables
and a Theory of Takeover

2.1 INTRODUCTION

In this chapter I shall set out a theory of takeovers based upon comparisons of the financial and stock market performance of firms taken over and firms not taken over. I am not attempting to simply discriminate between the two groups on whatever basis proves statistically significant,* but rather hope to provide economic justification for the inclusion of various variables which theoretically should operate to determine the causes of takeover. Only then can meaningful conclusions with respect to the theory of the firm be drawn from the statistical testing procedures employed in chapters 3 and 4.

2.2 THE VALUATION RATIO

Defined earlier as the ratio of the stock market value of the firm's capital over the book value of the firm's assets, the valuation ratio forms an integral part of Robin Marris's managerial theory of the firm.† By viewing the constraints on managerial behaviour in terms of a desire for security which competes with the achievement of a given objective, a primary

---

* We shall discuss this point further in section 5.3 where we summarise the results and conclusions for the various models employed in this study.

† More recently an allied hypothesis was put forward by Gort (1969). He argued that mergers occur because of differences in valuation of assets between buyers and sellers and attributes changes in valuation to rapid changes in stock prices or when technical change is great. He attempts to test this proposition in a cross-section study of industry merger rates. For a critical analysis of this work see Hindley (1972).

source of the threat to managerial security is provided by the likelihood that a given set of financial policies will result in the firm being taken over. Marris postulated a theory of takeover in terms of subjective valuation discrepancies between the value of the firm to the raider and the value the market places on it. Where a positive discrepancy exists between the raider's and the market's assessment, takeover will occur. The theory as it stands is not operational since the raider's valuation of the firm is a non-observable parameter. The theory is restated by Marris in terms of a probability function such that the lower the valuation ratio of a firm the greater will be the probability that a raider with a positive valuation discrepancy will come forward and hence the greater the probability that the firm will be taken over. The theory is now in a form where it is capable of being tested by suitable comparisons between the valuation ratios of acquired and non-acquired firms.

In addition to its role as a constraint on managerial behaviour in Marris's theory of the firm, the inclusion of the valuation ratio as a determinant of the probability of takeover can be examined from the raider's point of view. Assuming a firm wishes to expand its operation, it can either set up a new plant to its requirements or acquire an existing firm with suitable attributes. While the supply of suitable firms may be limited, the latter course can have several advantages. Not only does the raider succeed in removing a competitor as well as possibly reaching additional markets and enhancing its pool of managerial skills, but it may also be able to acquire a given set of assets cheaply, because of the existence of a large number of firms whose assets are valued on the market below their book value. Purely in terms of an investment decision by potential raiders, the lower a firm's valuation ratio the more attractive it becomes to acquire as part of their expansion plans.

Because the valuation ratio is determined in the stock market,* its level is based not only on the market's evaluation of its past performance (e.g. profits, growth and retentions policy) and present state (e.g. size and liquidity), but also on the market's expectations of its future. Thus, two firms with identical

---

* Although containing both measures of book value and market value, the valuation ratio is primarily market determined in the sense that the numerator is the most highly variable component.

records and size and liquidity positions but with one valued lower on the market than the other will be subject to differing probabilities of takeover – the lower valued firm facing the greater threat.

2.3 SIZE (NET ASSETS)

It is anticipated that the size of a firm will affect the likelihood that it will be taken over – the large firm being relatively safer than the small. This expectation of a negative sign relating size to the probability of takeover is based on two institutional observations. First, it is nearly always the case that the raider is significantly larger than the firm it acquires. Thus a large firm would face fewer potential raiders than a small firm and thereby have a smaller chance of being taken over. Furthermore, to acquire a large company involves greater risks to the raider and increases the difficulties involved in integrating it into the raider's existing structure. Second, to acquire a large company as opposed to a small one, places greater strains on the sources of finance of the purchase whether it be on the liquidity position of the raider when cash is involved or the market's willingness to accept additional equity or convertible loan stock (and the potential strains arising through increased gearing when this latter payments practice is used) if those are chosen as the method of payment. Possibly serving to obscure this size – takeover relationship is the evidence previously presented by Ma (1960) that mortality is higher in old firms and old firms tend to be larger than young firms.

2.4 THE PROFIT RATE

To the extent the valuation ratio is influenced by the past profit performance of a firm, the inclusion of the profit rate as a determinant of the probability of takeover is an alternative specification of the functional relationship. The profit rate provides an indicator of the success of the existing management of a firm and if the past record is poor then presumably a different set of management could earn a greater rate of return on the given assets. It is not independent of the valuation ratio because the raider's calculations concerning potential profitability of an acquired firm are not based on the expected return on the acquired net asset value but on the expected return relative to the cost of the acquisition. Furthermore, the market determination of the valuation ratio will to some extent be based upon the firm's past profit record. Only if a poor profit record depresses the valuation ratio sufficiently to make the likely cost of the firm (including the bid premium) in relation to its potential profitability under the raider's control attractive, will the takeover bid occur. At the extreme, a company making losses and facing the possibility of bankruptcy would become a takeover candidate* as its performance would undoubtedly result in a low and therefore attractive valuation ratio to a potential raider. The above reasoning forms the basis of Marris's argument for relying solely on the valuation ratio as the constraint on his specified objective function. He assumes that seeking high rates of growth which necessarily involves the sacrifice of profits below the profit maximising rate of return will directly tend to depress the valuation ratio thereby inviting the threat of takeover.

There will be a competing influence tending to confound the negative influence profits and consequently the valuation ratio have on the probability of takeover. Marris's original theory of takeover was based on the subjective valuation discrepancy of the raider and the stock market. If the poor profit record was the result of bad management then it is possible that even a very low valuation ratio of a firm is unattractive to the raider. This could occur if the bad management caused the assets of the firm to have no value to any potential raider (either because they were established to produce a product for which there was no demand or if they were allowed to deteriorate faster than the rate of depreciation) even though they retained some positive value on the books.† Also, if the poor profits were partly the result of a bad record of labour

---

* See Dewey (1961) and the footnote on page 19 above for a discussion of the assertion that takeovers are simply an alternative to bankruptcy.

† This belongs to the general class of measurement error problems with the valuation ratio and other financial variables. They may also stem from undervalued assets on the firm's books and differences between firm's accounting practices although to the extent the accounting procedures vary between industries and are fairly comparable within industries, the industry analysis of chapters 3 and 4 will alleviate this problem. Aside from recognising these potential sources of bias there is little one can do to remove them.

relations by the firm's management, unless the potential raider thought it could improve on the strike record, and that would probably be very difficult, the firm could remain an unattractive purchase no matter how great the apparent possibilities for improving on the firm's rate of return were it to be acquired cheaply. Herein lies a source of 'noise' to the posited profit and valuation ratio relationships and explains why a firm could survive for a number of years with low profits and a low valuation ratio without being taken over.*

2.5 THE GROWTH RATE

It is anticipated that the firm's growth rate of net assets will negatively influence the probability that it is taken over in a manner analogous to the expected role of profits and the probability of takeover. That is, the past growth record of a firm is expected to affect the probability that the firm is taken over through its influence on the valuation ratio. This is based on the notion that the market values a firm according to its expectations about the firm's future growth rate of earnings. Thus both its earnings record and its growth rate should provide different sorts of indicators of the past performance of the firm and hence a basis for the market to assess its value.

Marris has noted the possibility that firms attempting to maximise their growth rate may become takeover candidates because of the choice of an 'excessive' growth target caused loss of control and consequently failure to meet the profits constraint imposed through the valuation ratio.† Such a firm would be in a much stronger defensive position than one with low profits and low growth as the former could lower its growth rate and as a consequence increase its profitability‡ while

---

* We shall discuss this point in detail in the conclusion of chapter 3 since several authors have placed widely different interpretations on the existence of an imperfect valuation ratio–takeover relationship.

† Marris (1964) pp 123 and 259.

‡ This corresponds to the argument developed by Penrose (1959). However, it has been suggested by Eatwell (1971) p. 409 that the low observed correlation between growth and profitability is due to other factors which influence the relationship which may vary between industries, over time, and between different types of firms. By implication, any given firm, at a given point in time, would still face the Penrose trade-off between profits and growth.

the latter has no such option. More recently Marris has argued that survival is dependent upon adopting a growth maximising policy* and that firms which do otherwise (e.g. maximise profits) will be those which fail to survive. While I am not intending here to examine this assertion, this view is consistent with the treatment of the growth rate and the profit rate in this study, (i.e. as separate influences on the probability of takeover but associated through their role as factors affecting the market's determination of the valuation ratio).

2.6 THE RETENTION RATIO

It is expected that the choice of retention ratio (and hence dividend pay out ratio) by management would affect the probability of takeover again by way of its influence on the valuation ratio. Not only does the market have a positive preference for dividends, but an increase in the pay out ratio (i.e. a fall in the retention ratio) is usually seen as indicative of the management's expectation of an improvement in future earnings. For similar reasons, low or falling dividend ratios would tend to depress the valuation ratio. Furthermore, firms making very low profits would need to retain a very large proportion of after tax earnings simply to provide capital for replacement investment to stay in operation. Thus, not only by itself would the retention ratio be expected to affect the probability of takeover, but also it would be expected to act as a 'shifter' to the profits effect, both operating by way of the valuation ratio on the probability of takeover.

2.7 THE LIQUIDITY RATIO

A further influence on the probability of takeover is the firm's liquidity position. It is obvious that very liquid firms will be attractive takeover candidates at low valuation ratios, especially during periods of tight credit. Furthermore, a highly liquid firm would presumably not command a healthy market valuation as it would be sitting on cash or marketable securities that could be made available for profitable capital investments either to expand the output of its main product or diversify. The illiquid firm would presumably be doing precisely that

* See Marris (1968).

through the use of its available cash flow and debt. Certainly a large section of the market would approve of such policies (providing the debt did not reach a dangerous level and was not used to finance current losses) and reward the firm with a 'safe' valuation ratio.

It is likely however that the very poorly performing firm in terms of profits would also have a low liquidity position, requiring its cash reserves to service its loan stock, undertake some replacement capital investment and possibly show face with some sort of token dividend. This effect would, however, be felt by way of the profits variable, but, to the extent that it was present, would serve to obscure the basic relationship between the liquidity ratio and the probability of takeover.

2.8 THE INDUSTRIAL SETTING

As indicated in the previous chapter, the conditions operating in a particular industry will affect the probability of takeover (e.g. growth of demand, concentrations, etc.). However, the firm can only over a long period of time through diversification affect its industrial classification. Since a certain emphasis of this study is on considering the characteristics of the firm which the management control and the probability of takeover, the effect the industry class has on the probability of takeover within it, is only of descriptive interest. It would be misleading, however, to use this as a justification for ignoring the industry differences in the takeover rate and performance, and concentrating on the empirical verification of aggregate theoretical relationships as set out in this chapter. Because of the large inter-industry variations in each of the variables considered, a possibly overwhelming volume of 'noise' would be introduced, serving to confound the aggregate statistical relationships. Such 'noise' is certainly attributable to the industry characteristics, but since the vast majority of takeovers occur within the same or similar industries, it is the performance of the firm with respect to similar firms in the same industry which will single it out as a takeover candidate. The question asked is whether a firm is undervalued by the market for a given set of possibilities facing all firms in the industry and not whether a firm possesses a low valuation ratio as compared to all firms in the industrial population. For instance, a firm with a valuation ratio of

0·6 would be above the industry median if it were a shipping company but less than half that of the industry median if it were in the entertainments industry.* Furthermore, managers would be comparing their performance relative to firms in the same line, and raiders (except for the conglomerates) would be scrutinising firms on the basis of performance or cheapness relative to similar potential acquisitions.

The necessity of undertaking an examination of takeovers on an industry basis exists for all the variables discussed in this chapter both for reasons of accuracy of theoretical *and* statistical specification. In a low growth industry relatively (with respect to all firms in the industrial population) low valuation ratios, low growth rates, low profit rates, low retention ratios and high liquidity ratios could all be safe, while appearing to indicate a high risk of takeover if compared to firms in a high growth industry or even in the aggregate relationship. Furthermore, what may be a large dominant firm of £20m net assets in one industry could be undersized relative to the scale economies available in another industry.

2.9 SUMMARY

In this chapter I have set out briefly the anticipated theoretical relationships for the primary financial and stock-market variables to be employed in the statistical examination to follow. Nothing has been said concerning the functional form of any of the relationships, whether they are linear or curved, or the appropriate lag structure of the response. These are matters to be determined empirically rather than theoretically and as such will be considered when the models are formally constructed and tested in the next two chapters.

The primary emphasis in this chapter has been on the way in which the characteristics of the firm would affect its likelihood of being taken over. Of particular interest is the valuation ratio since it reflects not only the purchase price of the firm, but also incorporates the joint effects of the other financial variables of the firm. Three conclusions may be drawn from this concerning the procedure to adopt to test the importance

---

* See appendix 2 table 2 for the mean and median values of each industry's performance for the various stock market and financial variables.

of the anticipated relationships. First, the valuation ratio's role is crucial to the takeover mechanism. Second, the other financial variables which influence the probability of takeover but whose effect may operate through the valuation ratio should be examined separately from the valuation ratio. Third, the analysis should be undertaken at the industry level so that the wide inter-industry variations in the variables are suppressed in order to examine the hypotheses concerning each variable as relative to firms in a similar industrial situation.

3 Linear Probability Models of Takeovers I:

Industry Analysis of the Valuation Ratio and Size

3.1 INTRODUCTION

In this chapter I shall develop and test various formulations of the first of two basic models of takeovers employing two variables discussed in the previous chapter. This first model investigated is based on the anticipated inverse relationship between the valuation ratio and the probability that a firm will be taken over. The valuation ratio and the financial variables are included in separate models since it was expected that the effect of the latter would be felt through the valuation ratio. I shall investigate a number of relationships based on various possible formulations of the valuation ratio and size, a variable not expected to be correlated with the valuation ratio. Finally, each of the 67 industries will be treated separately since it is expected that it is the indicators of the firm's performance relative to comparable firms in the same industry which single it out as a takeover candidate. In this way, the specification of the model is improved such that the variations attributable solely to the industry class will be removed thereby giving the variables a greater chance to capture the posited dependence of the probability of takeover on each.

3.2 THE MODEL

The valuation ratio presents not only the most interesting theoretical relationship associated with the probability of takeover, but also the most difficult to specify. As noted earlier,

56

the theory put forward by Marris is based on the presence of a positive discrepancy between a potential raider's valuation of a firm and the market's valuation. Where such exists, takeover should occur. While the potential raider's valuation of a firm is not observable, the theory can be made operational by treating the relationship as a probability function. Thus, the lower the valuation ratio of a firm, the greater likelihood it will be taken over.

Distinct problems remain, however, in the measurement of a firm's valuation ratio. Since it is defined in terms of the market value of the firm divided by the book value or alternatively, the price of the ordinary voting shares over the net assets per share, it is obvious that a different valuation ratio exists for every market price that prevailed over the period. Furthermore, the denominator is only an accurate reflection of the book value of the firm on the day the firm closed its accounts for the year. Since it appeared that raiders timed their bid with respect to the publication of the accounts of a potential acquisition, it would seem plausible that any underestimate of the firm's book value which did not reflect growth that may have occurred between the last accounts and the offer would not be serious since the raider appears to base his decision on the best available information (i.e. the state of the firm as of the last accounting period). As far as the choice of the 'correct' numerator, presumably one desires to use that price which the raider based his decision whether or not to make the offer The theory gives us no further indication except that it should be a price sometime prior to the offer. The solution adopted was to employ three measures of the valuation ratio for firms taken over: V_{1a} – the valuation ratio in the year prior to the offer with the annual low share price in the numerator; V_{1b} – the valuation ratio in the year prior to the offer with the average of the annual high and low share price in the numerator; and V_{1c} – the valuation ratio in the year of the offer with the annual low share price in the numerator.

In order to make comparisons of these measures of the valuation ratio with firms which have not been taken over it was necessary to determine some representative level of the valuation ratio for these survivors. Consequently, two possibilities will be considered: V_{0a} – the average valuation ratio over all available years using the annual low share prices in the numerators; and V_{0b} – the average valuation ratio measured using the average of the annual high and low share prices in the numerators. In order to explore the possibility of a non linear relationship between the valuation ratio and takeover, logarithmic values of the above formulations will also be used.

Because of the long time period covered in this study, four possibilities exist that may tend to obscure the valuation ratio relationship. Since the hypothesis I wish to examine is framed in terms of the firm's performance, not only relative to the industry class, but also at a point in time, it is assumed that the raider chooses the most attractive takeover opportunity when he makes an offer. Thus the firm's attractiveness (or cheapness in terms of the valuation ratio) is relative to the other available takeover opportunities at the time the offer is made. No difficulties exist with employing the measures of the valuation ratio above if the relationship remains relatively stable through-out the period, (i.e. the probability that a firm in a given industry with a given valuation ratio will be taken over remains unchanged throughout the period). The first possibility is that trends in the stock market could alter the critical level of the valuation ratio which signalled a firm was going to be taken over. For instance, during the 1967–9 takeover boom, the EXTEL Security Value Index doubled from 200 in November 1966 to over 400 in January 1969.* If this affected all firm's share prices, the poorest performers could find their valuation ratios rising even though the probability that they would be taken over remain unchanged. Second, during a boom period of takeover activity a 'band wagon' effect and pressures to maintain their market share could cause raiders to adjust upward the level of valuation ratio that would prompt them to make an offer. Third, both the above mentioned effects could maintain raiders' desires to make takeovers within an industry, even though both the falling supply of acquirable firms resulting from past concentration through takeovers and market speculation by sectors on potential takeover candidates to reap the bid premium, caused valuation ratios of the surviving firms to rise. Finally, a learning

* See appendix 2 table 1.

effect by surviving firms that takeovers may be prompted by the possession of undervalued property assets could cause them to revalue more often. If so, a cause of takeovers in the earlier part of the period could be suspended in the latter part so that at first firms with high valuation ratios (i.e. with an artificially low denominator) would be observed to be taken over but as learning progressed and revaluations occurred, lower and lower levels would be necessary to provide the raider with a given requisite return on the acquisition.

The solution adopted to remove these possibilities was to specify the model in terms of the relative hypothesis described in the previous paragraph. That is, the valuation ratio measures, V_{1a}, V_{1b}, and V_{1c} were divided by the average of the industry for the year in which the takeover occurred (VA_{1a}, VA_{1b}, and VA_{1c}) appropriately measured using the same definition of the numerator as the acquired firm's valuation ratios. The valuation ratio for the non-taken over firms were divided by the industry average for all years (VA_0) appropriately measured. In this way the hypothesis that it was the relative cheapness of the firm at the time of the acquisition that caused the takeover could be tested removing any possibility of bias entering in the way described above. The surviving firm's valuation ratios were similarly normalised in order to make them comparable to the proportionate variable constructed for the acquired firms.

To these various formulations of the valuation ratio relationship is added firm size measured as net assets at the accounting date prior to the offer if the firm was taken over (S_1) or the average size over the period if it was not, (S_0). Unlike the other financial variables discussed in the previous chapter it was not anticipated that the firm's size would influence the valuation ratio.* As with the valuation ratio, size was alternatively employed as a ratio to the industry average size for the relevant year if the firm was taken over (SA_1) and relative to the industry average for all years if it was not, (SA_0).

A dummy dependent variable, T, is used in regressions run on the above variables taking a value of 1 if the firm was taken over and 0 otherwise. This technique is known as a linear

---

* Singh and Whittington (1968) p. 67 find no linear correlation between size and the valuation ratio.

probability function and has been commonly* employed
where there is a dichotomous, all or nothing response to given
values of the independent variable. I chose the linear probability
function to test the hypothesis at the industry level because
its interpretation is closely related to the theoretical formulation – i.e. that the level of the valuation ratio inversely
affects the probability that a firm will be taken over. With the
linear probability function, the conditional expectation of the
dependent variable given the values of the independent
variables may be interpreted as the conditional probability
that the event occurs. The calculated values of the dependent
variable from the parameter estimates using regression
techniques then are estimates of this conditional probability.
There are however several problems with the use of this technique. The disturbance term will not have a constant variance,
for it will be varying with the values of the valuation ratio and
thus violating the classical assumption of homoscedasticity.†
The expected values of the parameter estimates would remain
unbiased but there could be bias in the estimated value and
they will have needlessly large sample variances as therefore
would the predictions.

A second difficulty concerns the interpretation of the
calculated values as conditional probabilities since they can
lie outside the interval 0 to 1. This is not critical since their
interpretation can easily be restricted to values within the
meaningful range 0 to 1 as only the extreme values of the
independent variables will tend to produce calculated values
outside this interval. For instance, only very high values
of the valuation ratio could produce conditional probabilities
of takeover of less than 0 and it would subtract little to interpret
this as a firm which was immune from the threat of takeover.

An alternative technique and that adopted by Singh (1971)
in his study of takeovers is discriminant analysis.‡ While this

---

* For two economic examples of the use of the linear probability function
see Orcutt et al. (1961) and Lee (1964).

† For a demonstration of this characteristic of the linear probability function
see Goldberger (1965) pp. 248–55.

‡ For other economic examples of the use of discriminant analysis see
Durand (1941), Tintner (1952), Blood and Baker (1958), and Ladd
(1968).

technique has been shown by R. A. Fisher and G. W. Ladd to be formally equivalent to the linear probability function,* its interpretation is somewhat cumbersome when repeatedly applied to a large number of industries.

The definitions of the variables used to examine the influence of the valuation ratio and size on whether or not the firm was taken over are summarised below:

T = a dummy variable taking the value of 1 if the firm was taken over and 0 if it was not.

if $T = 0$ then

V_{0a} = the valuation ratio averaged over all available years measured using the annual low share prices in the numerators

V_{0b} = the valuation ratio averaged over all available years measured using the average of the annual highs and lows in the numerators.

$\log V_{0a}$ = logarithmic values of the variable defined above

$\log V_{0b}$ = logarithmic values of the variable defined above

V_{0a}/VA_{0a} = V_{0a} divided by the average of the valuation ratios of all firms in the industry over all years measured using the annual low share prices in the numerators

V_{0b}/VA_{0b} = V_{0b} divided by the average of the valuation ratios of all firms in the industry over all years measured using the average of the annual high and low share prices in the numerators

S_0 = size (net assets) of the firm averaged over all available years

S_0/SA_0 = S_0 divided by the size of all firms in the averaged over all available years

if $T = 1$ then

V_{1a} = the valuation ratio in the year prior to the offer with the annual low share price in the numerator

* Fisher (1944) and Ladd (1966).

V_{1b} = the valuation ratio in the year prior to the offer with the average of the annual high and low share prices in the numerator

V_{1c} = the valuation ratio in the year of the offer with the annual low share price in the numerator

$\log V_{1a}$ = logarithmic value of the variable defined above

$\log V_{1b}$ = logarithmic value of the variable defined above

$\log V_{1c}$ = logarithmic value of the variable defined above

V_{1a}/VA_{1a} = V_{1a} divided by the average of the valuation ratios of all firms in the industry in the year prior to the offer with the annual low share prices in the numerators

V_{1b}/VA_{1b} = V_{1b} divided by the average of the valuation ratios of all firms in the industry in the year prior to the offer with the average of the annual high and low share prices in the numerators

V_{1c}/VA_{1c} = V_{1c} divided by the average of the valuation ratios of all firms in the industry in the year of the offer with the annual low share price in the numerators

S_1 = size (net assets) of the firm at the accounting period prior to the offer

S_1/SA_1 = S_1 divided by the average size of all firms in the industry for the year in which S_1 was measured.

Using these variables, the following 9 regression equations were derived to be run on each industry using comparable measures of the valuation ratio and size.

1) if $T = 0$: V_{0a}, S_0; if $T = 1$: V_{1a}, S_1
2) if $T = 0$: V_{0b}, S_0; if $T = 1$: V_{1b}, S_1
3) if $T = 0$: V_{0a}, S_0; if $T = 1$: V_{1c}, S_1
4) if $T = 0$: V_{0a}/VA_{0a}, S_0/SA_0; if $T = 1$: V_{1a}/VA_{1a}, S_1/SA_1
5) if $T = 0$: V_{0b}/VA_{0b}, S_0/SA_0; if $T = 1$: V_{1b}/VA_{1b}, S_1/SA_1
6) if $T = 0$: V_{0a}/VA_{0a}, S_0/SA_0; if $T = 1$: V_{1c}/VA_{1c}, S_1/SA_1
7) if $T = 0$: $\log V_{0a}$; if $T = 1$: $\log V_{1a}$

8)   if $T = 0$: log V_{0b}; if $T = 1$: log V_{1b}
9)   if $T = 0$: log V_{0a}; if $T = 1$: log V_{1c}

3.3   RESULTS

A sample of the results appear in tables 3.1 and 3.2 and a summary of the results for all industries appears in table 3.3 below. Table 3.1 contains the full results for the furnishing industry, selected because it is illustrative of an industry well behaved according to the hypothesis but nevertheless not untypical. Table 3.2 presents the complete results for two

TABLE 3.1

Regressions on the Furnishing Industry
Dummy Dependent Variable on the Valuation Ratio and Size

Regression no.	Constant	Valuation ratio	Size	F	$\bar{R}^2$
1	0·62956 (0·07524)	−0·24433 (0·05343)	−0·00191* (0·00198)	8·35647	0·15599
2	0·56742 (0·08217)	−0·18393 (0·05659)	−0·00216* (0·00207	4·51194	0·07719
3	0·57980 (0·07787)	−0·19580 (0·05385)	−0·00211* (0·00204)	5·70961	0·10327
4	0·33496 (0·07099)	−0·16184 (0·07030)	−0·01117* (0·00940)	2·71637	0·03635
5	0·36780 (0·06960)	−0·18962 (0·06494)	−0·01047* (0·00927)	3·79628	0·06294
6	0·31759 (0·07084)	−0·13854 (0·06837)	−0·01136* (0·00945)	2·29675	0·02560
7	0·34004 (0·03742)	−0·37305 (0·05639)		43·76380	0·26812
8	0·35901 (0·04151)	−0·30343 (0·06717)		20·40530	0·13901
9	0·34704 (0·03911)	−0·33581 (0·05921)		32·15760	0·20920

Note: standard errors of the associated parameter estimates appear below each in brackets. Also, only those parameter estimates marked with an asterisk (*) fail to emerge as significant at the 5 per cent level.

TABLE 3.2

Selected Regression Results All Industries – Valuation Ratio and Size

Industry no.	Regression no.	Constant	Valuation ratio	Size	F	$\bar{R}^2$	N
1	1	0·57850	−0·19138*	0·00293*	3·80451	0·08291	82
	7	0·32050	−0·32271		15·18750	0·13854	
2	1	0·77897	−0·36084*	0·00049*	7·18920	0·13252	115
	7	0·39069	−0·42069		27·18050	0·17963	
3	1	0·79476	−0·25505	−0·00158*	2·41089*	0·06566	46
	7	0·52279	−0·40875		11·75090	0·17490	
4	1	0·71265	−0·28993	−0·00277*	9·87853	0·16686	128
	7	0·36150	−0·41183		51·06040	0·27708	
5	1	0·27444	−0·00629*	−0·00923*	1·56013*	0·00381	178
	7	0·28936	−0·20014		29·53000	0·13395	
6	1	0·59617	−0·15249	−0·00364*	7·10045	0·07111	226
	7	0·40190	−0·24159		28·56180	0·10517	
7	1	0·73617	−0·29648	−0·00095*	3·50619	0·07201	84
	7	0·39246	−0·35347		12·94940	0·11532	
8	1	0·45275	−0·12126	−0·00442*	5·62490	0·06474	186
	7	0·29800	−0·22663		30·17810	0·13156	
9	1	0·42755	−0·01655	0·00021*	1·73575*	0·00428	281
	7	0·44570	−0·27339		54·97250	0·15861	

10	1	0·46322	−0·15161	−0·00203*	10·66440	0·07930	325
	7	0·27336	−0·25432		52·78680	0·13515	
11	1	0·70031	−0·38476	−0·00148*	10·52400	0·16070	144
	7	0·29838	−0·32838		32·97360	0·17702	
12	3ᵃ	0·39809	−0·03444*	−0·00154*	0·99276*	−0·00410	250
	7	0·35278	−0·23821		35·93260	0·11951	
13	1ᵇ	0·25328*	0·01835*	−0·00281*	0·22030*	−0·18090	34
	7	0·24709	−0·10617*		0·68518*	−0·04023	
14	1	0·43084	−0·05444	0·00155*	4·49842	0·04832	187
	7	0·40646	−0·35854		57·04720	0·22742	
15	1	0·58327	−0·28458	−0·00245	6·65575	0·10577	135
	7	0·26487	−0·36643		26·40060	0·15308	
16	1	0·64764	−0·17279	−0·00599*	6·83101	0·06356	243
	7	0·42671	−0·33159		39·04140	0·13227	
17	1	0·42294	−0·02283	−0·00022*	2·58893*	0·01220	305
	7	0·39256	−0·26310		47·18300	0·12903	
18	1	0·70912	−0·25109*	0·00220*	1·68112*	0·03065	33
	7	0·04579	−0·15837		4·41918	0·06830	
19	1	0·83059	−0·68192	−0·00205*	4·03746	0·15274	45
	7	0·21734	−0·33784		12·61130	0·19081	
20	1	0·75294	−0·39591	−0·00479*	7·79156	0·19695	79
	7	0·28402	−0·35427		30·00910	0·26175	
21	1	0·62763	−0·04835*	−0·00088*	2·71753*	−0·06473	60
	7	0·43963	−0·28969		5·60684	0·05671	

Table 3.2 – *cont.*

Industry no.	Regression no.	Constant	Valuation ratio	Size	F	$\bar{R}^2$	N
22	1	0.62957	−0.24433	−0.00191*	8.35647	0.15599	114
	7	0.34004	−0.37305		43.76380	0.26812	
23	1	0.40390	−0.07055*	−0.00158*	1.79075*	0.00951	143
	7	0.32381	−0.17550		18.72350	0.10470	
24	1	0.63680	−0.17415	−0.00051*	1.69522*	0.02520	42
	7	0.42243	−0.21227		7.14233	0.10908	
25	1	0.76791	−0.28663	−0.00243*	13.11780	0.14010	217
	7	0.41580	−0.35315		49.18870	0.17862	
26	1	0.60393	−0.28618	0.00173*	7.96240	0.13632	126
	7	0.28613	−0.23437		22.20800	0.13821	
27	1	0.60748	−0.20227	−0.00918*	3.34822	0.09742	56
	7	0.34474	−0.26046		9.14671	0.11318	
28	1	0.71687	−0.17948	−0.00057*	4.12697	0.09483	80
	7	0.50222	−0.26705		13.62260	0.12685	
29	1	0.36676	−0.01717*	−0.00046*	1.37804*	0.00098	137
	7	0.36112	−0.19918		19.69560	0.11439	
30	1	0.48684	−0.05274	−0.00136*	2.03922*	0.01679	124
	7	0.45718	−0.24242		16.66170	0.10574	
31	1	0.79522	−0.24598	−0.00346*	3.53133	0.11651	50
	7	0.48604	−0.28970		10.19370	0.14080	

32	1	0·56662	−0·24878*	−0·01082*	1·59627*	0·01584	49
	7	0·29039	−0·26731		7·58774	0·10236	
33	1	0·40769	−0·04754*	0·00055*	1·41477*	0·00578	42
	7	0·36963	−0·19252		13·64820	0·21712	
34	1	0·66756	−0·27064	0·00156*	7·11429	0·14655	101
	7	0·30339	−0·36837		40·93800	0·27825	
35	4c	0·42083	−0·03080*	−0·01539*	1·40227*	0·00299	70
	7	0·45892	−0·15662		9·43488	0·09602	
36	1	0·88600	−0·19306	−0·00398	8·48937	0·11513	166
	7	0·60497	−0·30847		23·34010	0·11452	
37	1	0·76459	−0·45021	0·00316*	6·09272	0·18240	64
	7	0·31698	−0·41675		22·95960	0·24668	
38	5c	0·37185	−0·03598*	−0·02666*	1·93283*	0·01000	178
	7	0·47751	−0·23255		32·45970	0·14542	
39	1	0·72642	−0·26664	−0·00427*	5·44587	0·10605	104
	7	0·40719	−0·35257		24·23220	0·17612	
40	1	0·46526	−0·00114*	−0·00945*	0·81696*	−0·02168	73
	7	0·51371	−0·16871		14·91060	0·15028	
41	5c	0·46457	−0·00110*	−0·01144	3·13715	0·02144	255
	7	0·56630	−0·18392		36·48990	0·11955	
42	1	0·73085	−0·11612	−0·01679	4·96080	0·11005	88
	7	0·53033	−0·20184		12·49690	0·10462	
43	5	0·42928	−0·09863*	−0·06052	2·54277*	0·07167	49
	7	0·52837	−0·06146*		0·29785*	−0·03599	

TABLE 3.2 – *cont.*

Industry no.	Regression no.	Constant	Valuation ratio	Size	F_t	$\bar{R}^2$	N
44	5^c	0·77424	-0·24794*	-0·08024	2·98322	0·09175	51
	7	0·63742	-0·26447		6·01338	0·07295	
45	1	0·59157	-0·09495	-0·00550*	2·14330*	0·05349	43
	7	0·43232	-0·14800		7·73007	0·11759	
46	1	0·78891	-0·42486	-0·00045*	7·83677	0·19606	80
	7	0·13891	-0·45487		31·76250	0·27115	
47	1	0·41138	-0·01135*	0·00093*	1·22773*	-0·00218	146
	7	0·44148	-0·18743		22·97900	0·12564	
48	5^d	0·57216	-0·13313	-0·02714	4·47437	0·11573	74
	7	0·64368	-0·16692		11·51860	0·11397	
49	1	0·76126	-0·19932	-0·00276*	6·87671	0·17762	77
	7	0·50059	-0·35837		27·00110	0·24511	
50	1	0·76236	-0·19986	-0·00178*	5·38542	0·11900	90
	7	0·51254	-0·26433		18·12500	0·15194	
51	5^c	0·34662	-0·01135*	-0·03452*	1·57338*	0·00850	88
	7	0·40792	-0·12421		11·10290	0·09375	
52	3	0·71143	-0·36355	-0·00215*	2·40463*	0·07798	38
	9	0·36524	-0·43869		11·01450	0·19174	

							N
53	1	0·65465	−0·19225	−0·00252*	2·40565*	0·02893	108
	7	0·37233	−0·25660		13·84090	0·09881	
54	1[b]	0·48724	0·00337	−0·00286*	1·60987*	0·00379	218
	7	0·42293	−0·15223		15·38520	0·06649	
55	1	0·72626	−0·15554	−0·00232*	3·06434	0·05343	92
	7	0·50934	−0·22390		12·15150	0·09938	
56	1	0·60527	−0·21048	−0·00056*	6·16594	0·09763	134
	7	0·36411	−0·15109		11·30790	0·06495	
57	1	0·53018	−0·11305	−0·00355*	4·36304	0·06630	128
	7	0·37170	−0·17118		12·36930	0·07494	
58	1	0·40290	−0·00504*	−0·00078*	0·52134*	−0·11297	24
	7	0·38162	−0·08198*		2·42868*	0·01755	
59	1	0·38003	−0·00142*	−0·00024*	0·60063*	−0·02730	83
	7	0·40656	−0·13946		11·36620	0·10140	
61	1	0·38438	−0·00321*	−0·00084*	0·98514*	−0·00410	256
	7	0·40712	−0·25173		34·48480	0·11261	
62	1	0·42891	−0·04415	−0·00055*	2·82112	0·04041	106
	7	0·39244	−0·28226		35·52740	0·24029	
63	1	0·69633	−0·41194	−0·00203*	2·96695	0·06852	34
	7	0·36220	−0·30288*		3·16335	0·03308	
64	1[e]	0·15555*	0·40129	−0·00021*	2·52505*	0·08811	37
	7[e]	0·42905	0·06670*		0·15388*	−0·05252	

TABLE 3.2 – *cont.*

Industry no.	Regression no.	Constant	Valuation ratio	Size	F	$\bar{R}^2$	N
65	1	0·38839	−0·02424*	−0·00269*	1·07415*	−0·01140	69
	7	0·26097	−0·10507*		1·74470*	−0·00371	
66	4	0·44584	−0·00742*	−0·07305*	1·47240*	0·09609	44
	7	0·46729	−0·14227*		3·18319*	0·02619	
67	1	0·79040	−0·40597	−0·00339*	5·58991	0·22897	43
	7	0·38427	−0·42557		18·39790	0·27607	

[a] This was the only regression which had a negative parameter estimate in this industry. All forms were, however, insignificant.

[b] Regression 1 is illustrated as it is usually the 'best' form. In this industry all parameter estimates were insignificant and had the wrong sign.

[c] None of the regressions in this industry was significant but the regression shown had the highest F value.

[d] Regression 5 was the only form where the valuation ratio was significant.

[e] Regressions 1 and 7 are illustrated as they are usually the 'best' form. In this industry all regressions had parameter estimates of the valuation ratio of positive sign and all but 3 were significant.

Note: Those parameter estimates marked with an asterisk (*) fail to emerge as significant at the 5 per cent level.

regressions in each industry,* being those which demonstrate the effect of the valuation ratio most clearly. The summary in table 3.3 shows the proportion of the 66 industries† in which each variable proved to be both significant and possess the theoretically anticipated sign.

3.4 INTERPRETATION OF RESULTS AND CONCLUSIONS

In this section I shall initially discuss the results of the nine regressions run on the furnishing industry presented in table 3.1. This is offered purely for illustrative purposes as an aid to the interpretation of the results in table 3.2 which follows. The summary table of the results, table 3.3 will then be discussed with reference to the industry differences. Finally I shall sum up the conclusions that can be drawn from this section of the study.

Of primary interest in table 3.1 is that the parameter estimates of the valuation ratio are negative and significant at the 5 per cent level of probability in all nine regressions. This negative sign is in accordance with the theoretically anticipated

TABLE 3.3

Valuation Ratio Regressions – Summary

Regression no.	No. of industries with significant negative sign		Proportion of industries with significant negative sign (%)	
	valuation ratio	size	valuation ratio	size
1	39	5	59·1	7·6
2	17	5	25·8	7·6
3	29	5	43·9	7·6
4	4	11	6·1	16·7
5	11	10	16·7	15·2
6	2	12	3·0	18·2
7	59	—	89·4	—
8	42	—	63·6	—
9	55	—	83·3	—

* One regression was selected from regressions 1) to 6) and the other from the logarithmic formulations, regressions 7) to 9).
† Industry number 60, Insurance Brokers, was dropped in this analysis because it contained too few observations.

relationship between the valuation ratio and the likelihood of takeover. Furthermore, the intercept is positive and less than 1 in all cases. Because, by definition, both the valuation ratio and size must be positive, the predicted probability of takeover from the regression equations must be less than 1.* This is consistent with an interpretation of the regression equations as linear probability functions such that the predicted value of the dependent variable for any given level of valuation ratio is an estimate of the conditional probability that a firm with such a valuation ratio will be taken over. The predicted value does however take on values less than 0 at high levels of the valuation ratio and this is inconsistent with the meaning of probability. This is illustrated in the figure below where regression 1 for the furnishing industry is plotted with the valuation ratio and takeover input data.

Here at valuation ratios above 2.6 the predicted values become negative. Without difficulty one can retain the probability function interpretation by regarding the conditional probability of takeover for firms with valuation ratios greater than 2.6 as zero so that such firms could be regarded as safe from the threat of takeover. This does not however mean that empirically one will never observe a firm being taken over whose valuation ratio is greater than that denoted by the intersection of the regression line and the horizontal axis (i.e. where the estimated conditional probability of takeover is less than zero). This situation does in fact occur in the figure above where a firm is taken over with a pre-bid valuation ratio of 3.0.

With these regressions and those in the next chapter, one is looking for significant influences on the probability of takeover, and, in particular, it is theoretically anticipated that the valuation ratio should be an important factor. This is not to say that it will be the only factor for especially in cross-section analysis there will be manifold unspecified and unspecifiable influences affecting the relationship. The existence of a small number of firms for which the relationship fails to hold such

---

* Since size and log size were not significant they were dropped from the last three regressions for each industry. As a consequence, in the analysis of table 3.1 below we shall concentrate on the interpretation of the valuation takeover relationship.

that they get taken over when they would be expected to be safe, or survive with persistently low valuation ratios, only serves to indicate that other influences exist which can override valuation ratio considerations.* This does not in any way detract from the theoretically postulated and empirically verified hypothesis.

A comment is necessary on the meaning in this context of the corrected coefficient of determination ($\bar{R}^2$). While the F statistic provides a test of the hypothesis that no relationship exists between the valuation ratio and whether or not the firm is taken over, $\bar{R}^2$ is no longer to be interpreted as an indicator of the 'goodness of fit' of the regression line. To be sure, it is still the ratio of the sum of the squared deviations about the least-squares line to the total sum of squared deviations about the mean. Nevertheless, we can indicate the point with reference to figure 3.1. It is obvious that were there no overlap (i.e. a vertical line could be drawn passing through the two horizontal lines corresponding to 0 and 1 on the vertical axis at a particular level of valuation ratio such that all taken over firms had valuation ratios less than that level and all survivors had valuation ratios greater than that level, but horizontal variation existed within the two groups) we would have a perfect fit of the hypothesis in the sense that a critical level of the valuation ratio existed that determined perfectly and completely whether or not a firm would be taken over. Nevertheless, depending upon the amount of horizontal variation within the non-overlapping groups, $\bar{R}^2$ could be considerably below its maximum of 1. This situation is of particular importance given the natural tendency towards skewness of the distribution

---

* Two obvious examples of how the former could arise is through the 'reverse' takeover whereby firm A agrees to acquire the capital of firm B which is larger and therefore winds up controlling the joint capital of both. Here the roles of raider and acquired firm have been reversed. An associated second possibility occurs in voluntary takeovers, for example, brought about by the death of the owner of a family controlled firm. Here the takeover is really a sale and may have nothing to do with the firm's past performance. As I had no data on either, except to note that they occur, they remain possible explanations for 'perverse' observations. I have previously considered explanations for the survival of firms with persistently low valuation ratios in section 2.4 and will return to this point at the end of this chapter.

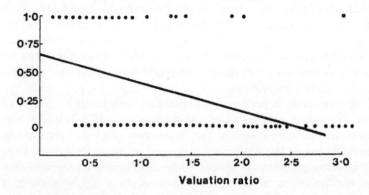

FIGURE 3.1 Industry 22, regression 1 – plotted valuation ratio takeover data.

of valuation ratios of surviving firms because the distribution is unbounded in a positive direction. Thus the reader should bear in mind that the value of $\bar{R}^2$ could severely underestimate the 'true' explanatory power of the estimated regression equations.*

The same interpretation of the results for the furnishing industry can be applied to the results in table 3.2 where two estimated regressions are presented for each industry. One regression was chosen from the first six and a second from the last three, being those for which the valuation ratio takes on the correct sign and is of greatest significance as indicated by the F statistic. In the first six regressions, regression 1 proved to offer the best explanation of whether or not a firm would be taken over in 56 out of the 66 industries. That is, the functional form which best separated the two groups was that where the

---

* One could construct an indicator of the goodness of fit based on the degree of overlap but for present purposes finding significant influences is sufficient to support the hypothesis. Discriminant analysis provides such an indicator of the explanatory power in terms of the degree of misclassification based on derived coefficients which in fact are proportional to the parameter estimates arrived at with the linear probability function. This indicator however requires that the two groups come from normal populations which with reference to both the definition of the valuation ratio (i.e. negative values are precluded while the positive range is theoretically unbounded) and by inspection of figure 3·1 will not be satisfied.

valuation ratio was measured with the annual low share price
in the numerator in the year prior to the offer when the firm
was taken over and as the average of the annual valuation
ratios measured with the low share price in the numerator
when it survived. That it should prove superior to regressions
2 or 3 is not surprising if the numerator in V_{1b} (the valuation
ratio with the mean share price in the year prior to the offer)
or V_{1c} (the valuation ratio with the low share price in the
numerator in the year of the offer) was picking up some pre-bid
speculation as the result of rumours leaked in the City. What
is disappointing is that attempts to improve the specification
of the model by relating the valuation ratios to the industry
average for the appropriate year if the firm was taken over,
were frustrated. In only 10 industries did these relative valuation ratios prove a superior measure to the form in regression 1.
However, in 8 of these 10 industries the valuation ratio proved
not to be significant. A possible explanation for this is that
despite variations in the market and within sectors of the market
there remained a fairly stable view of the nature of attractive
takeover candidates and thus the valuation ratio takeover
relationship remained stable throughout the period. However,
it is possible the relative valuation ratio relationship is being
obscured by the presence of a number of years in which share
prices within an industry were highly volatile resulting in a
number of firms with temporary but quite low valuation ratios.
By dividing the taken over firms' valuation ratios by VA_{0a}
which itself could be very low, one may be finding firms being
taken over with apparently above average valuation ratios.
Thus the method used to construct the relative valuation
ratios for taken over firms may be introducing sufficient
extraneous variation to the relationship due to the movements of
the stock market, to have a net effect in most industries of
detracting from the original valuation ratio relationship in
regressions 1 to 3.

Nevertheless, the results demonstrate that at least in a
majority of industries, the valuation ratio is a significant
determinant of whether or not a firm is taken over. Furthermore,
by inspection of table 3.2 it can be seen that the least-squares
line can be interpreted as a probability function (with the
qualification that high values of the valuation ratio will yield

calculated values of the conditional probability of takeover of less than zero). In all industries the intercept is less than 1 and all significant parameter estimates for the valuation ratio are negative,* so that not only is the conditional probability less than 1, but it declines as the valuation ratio increases.

The alternative formulation of regressions 7 to 9 where the logarithm of the valuation ratio is employed seems to offer an improvement on the results of regression 1. Regression 7 which involves an analogous form of the valuation ratio to regression 1 but with size omitted is in all but 10 industries a superior form of the relationship as indicated by both the F statistic and $\bar{R}^2$. In only one industry is regression 7 not the best form of the logarithmic relationship and in only 7 industries does the parameter estimate for log valuation ratio fail to emerge as significant. In all cases it takes on the expected negative sign.

Because the slope of the fitted logarithmic relationship is everywhere negative and decreases in absolute value as the valuation ratio increases, the superior results for regressions 7 to 9 would seem to indicate that as the valuation ratio decreases, the firm faces an ever increasing probability of takeover, reaching a maximum at the value of the intercept with the vertical axis (i.e. at a valuation ratio of zero). Certainly this is a possible interpretation of the results. It is, however, easy to see how the improved results emerged. The contraction in the scales resulting from taking logs of the valuation ratios clearly brought the high observations of the valuation ratio nearer the log linear regression line thereby improving both the F value and $\bar{R}^2$. Thus one should keep this reservation in mind when concluding that a superior form of the relationship is logarithmic.

The size variable emerged as significant and negative in only a small number of industries. This was probably to be expected from an examination of the aggregate grouped data on size and proportion of takeovers in table 1.8e. Thus in general it appeared that even quite large firms were subject to the same threat of takeover with a given valuation ratio as

---

* Indeed in all but two industries the parameter estimates for regression 1 take on the anticipated negative sign though some of these fail to emerge as significant at the 5 per cent level of probability.

small firms, perhaps only the handfull of giants experiencing some degree of safety because of their size. The constraints on finance and the limited supply of very large raiders that the negative expectation for the size variable was based does not emerge empirically. Nevertheless, when size is measured relative to the industry average for the appropriate year(s) as in regressions 4 to 6 it becomes significant and negative in a few more industries (see table 3.3). In general, the effect however is at best weak.

It will be remembered that the reason for running the regressions at the industry level was to remove the 'noise' generated through large inter-industry variations in the median value of various performance indicators. It was anticipated that this source of noise could serve to swamp the emergence of the underlying valuation ratio takeover relationship. Nevertheless, it was hoped it would be possible to comment upon the industry differences in the valuation ratio size take-over relationship that have emerged. In particular I wish to discover whether there are any common attributes of the twenty-four industries for which the valuation ratio in regression 1 failed to emerge as significant and of the twelve industries for which size proved significant in regression 6. To accomplish this I first ranked the industries by median growth rate, size, valuation ratio, profit rate, and proportion of takeovers. I then counted the number of non-significant regression co-efficients of the valuation ratio and the significant coefficients for size in each of 6 grouped rankings. Thus the first group contains the eleven industries with the lowest growth rate, the second contains the next highest eleven industries and so forth. This was done for all five industry characteristics above, and the results appear in table 3.4 and table 3.5. In each case the industry characteristics were ranked from lowest to highest.

The most noticeable point in table 3.4 is the absence of any strong tendency for the five industry characteristics to identify a common factor in the industries for which the valuation rato failed to emerge as significant. Thus while the median level of the valuation ratio is higher in growth industries than in fairly static industries, the valuation ratio takeover relationship seemed to have fit equally well in both. One might have expected the struggle for market share in low growth industries

TABLE 3.4

*Number of Non-significant Valuation ratio Coefficients (Regression 1)
for Ranked and Grouped Industries by Industry Characteristics*

Industry characteristics	Ranked industries						
	1–11	12–22	23–33	34–44	45–55	56–66	Total
Growth rate	5	3	5	2	4	5	24
Size	5	5	2	4	3	5	24
Valuation ratio	5	5	1	3	6	4	24
Profit rate	7	2	3	3	3	6	24
Proportion of Takeovers	4	6	3	3	3	5	24

TABLE 3.5

*Number of Significant size Coefficients (Regression 6) for Ranked and Grouped
Industries by Industry Characteristics*

Industry characteristics	Ranked industries						
	1–11	12–22	23–33	34–44	45–55	56–66	Total
Growth rate	1	3	4	0	1	3	12
Size	1	0	4	3	1	3	12
Valuation ratio	1	0	3	2	2	4	12
Profit rate	2	2	1	2	1	4	12
Proportion of Takeovers	1	0	1	1	2	7	12

to have suspended or at least obscured the valuation ratio
takeover relationship to a greater degree than in the high
growth industries where investment decisions whether internal
or external via takeover would possibly be more strongly
judged against expected rate of return. Thus in growth industries
one might have expected the valuation ratio to be a more consistently significant determinant of the probability of takeover.
The results, however, do not support this expectation. Similarly
the median size of the industry does not appear to explain the
failure of certain industries to fit the relationship established
elsewhere. Given that size in general failed to emerge as
significant in the industry regressions, one might still have

expected the industries whose median size was small to show the established relationship less clearly, as a raider whether within the industry or outside looking for expansion could acquire these small firms with possibly less regard for their market valuation. The failure of this characteristic of the industry to identify any common ground in the industries which do not fit the valuation ratio relationship is in this sense some additional confirmation that size, and hence potential financial constraints, fails to play an important role in the pattern of takeovers.

With the industry characteristics of median valuation ratio and median profit rate there is a slight tendency for the two extremes to embrace a greater number of industries which do not conform to the valuation ratio takeover relationship. Not only could these marginal differences have come about by chance, but also an explanation of why the extreme grouping(s) for the valuation ratio and the two end groups for the profit rate should display any greater tendency to fail to fit the relationship is not obvious. A breaking down of the relationship at the lower median values could possibly be understood in terms of some other motive (e.g. takeovers occurring as an alternative to widespread industry bankruptcies, the firms who get taken over performing as well or better than those which do not) overriding the normal valuation ratio takeover relationship, but this would not apply to both extremes. In any case, any effect is only at best slight.

Finally, it was anticipated that the industries experiencing the highest takeover rates could be more likely to have the observed takeover valuation ratio relationship obscured. This could have occurred if through the rapid increases in concentration that resulted from approximately half the firms being acquired,* there was an upward shift in the threshold level of valuation ratio that signalled the threat of takeover. Not only could the 'bargains' of the earlier concentration movement have been exhausted, but also market speculation on potential takeovers by industry and any effect on profitability of the increased concentration as well as a 'band wagon effect' by

---

* The 6th group ranked 56th to 66th ranged from over 46 per cent to nearly 61 per cent of the firms being taken over.

raiders not to be outdone by rivals in terms of market share, all could have pushed up the general level of valuation ratios over time and consequently obscured the relationship. This possibility does not appear to have occurred. There appears to be virtually no difference in the failure to conform to the valuation ratio takeover relationship and the industry takeover rate. In any case, if the reasoning above were substantiated by table 3.4 one would have expected regressions 4 through 6 (the set of regressions run with the valuation ratio measured as relative to the industry average for the appropriate year if the firm was taken over) to have performed better than they did. So in this sense the indecisive results in table 3.4 for the proportion of companies taken over in each industry and the failure of the valuation ratio takeover relationship are at least consistent.

In table 3.5 attempts were made to discover whether there was any common ground between the twelve industries for which size emerged as significant in regression 6. The most striking feature to emerge is the (fairly clear) tendency for those industries with the highest proportion of takeovers (i.e. group 6 with the 56th to 66th ranked industries) to be those in which size took on a significant negative sign. Thus in seven out of the eleven industries with the highest takeover rates, size proved to be a significant distinguishing characteristic of the taken over firm. I think the explanation for this is fairly obvious. In those industries experiencing rapid takeover activity the size gap between the raider and the acquired firm would be expected not only to be large, but also growing as more takeovers occurred. As regards the other four industry characteristics in table 3.5, no real clear cut pattern emerges to point to why in certain industries size became significant.*

I have previously noted that the linear probability function has been criticised on two grounds as an estimational technique; it can yield estimates of conditional probability outside the interval 0 to 1 and it violates the classical least-squares assumption of homoscedasticity. I have already dealt with the former,

---

* There is for both size and the valuation ratio an indication that in the lowest two groups, size is an even poorer distinguishing characteristic of the acquired and non-acquired firm. As an explanation for this is not immediately apparent, I shall simply note this in passing.

but some comment is necessary on the latter's effect on the results. While the least-squares estimates derived using this technique will still be unbiased and generally consistent, the formula for calculating the standard errors of the estimates will no longer hold. The effect of this error in the formula will be an underestimation of the standard errors of the parameter estimates. In the results that are presented, therefore, the use of the conventional formula for the standard error will cause us, at the margin, to accept as significant at the 95 per cent level, parameter estimates which are not in fact different from zero at this probability level. In any case, we have regarded parameter estimates at or very near the rule of thumb, two standard deviations from zero, as non-significant so that the effect of the heteroscedasticity is unlikely to seriously affect the broad conclusions drawn.

3.5 RESULTS AND THE THEORY OF THE FIRM

The results contained in this chapter for the valuation ratio model of takeovers represent a departure from two of the three related UK studies in this field. The pilot study undertaken prior to this work* found a highly significant inverse relationship between the valuation ratio and whether or not a firm was taken over using a random sample of 250 UK public quoted companies. The linear probability function estimational technique was also employed in that study. However, Ajit Singh's work in the area for the period 1948–60† failed to uncover corresponding results as contained in the pilot study and this chapter. While he did not include the valuation ratio in all stages of the analysis, he found it generally to be a poor discriminator between taken over and non-taken over firms. He found the mean values of the valuation ratio for the two groups to be significantly different but its ability to usefully discriminate between the two groups was very small both alone and in the presence of other financial variables.

The other related UK study employing the valuation ratio is by Gerald Newbould,‡ in which he examines the 1967–68

* Kuehn (1969).
† Singh (1971).
‡ Newbould (1970).

period of takeovers. He examined valuation ratios of 74 'victim firms' in the period in absolute terms and relative to the raiders'* and relative to the industrys'† average valuation ratios. He suggested that if a Marris type hypothesis is to be vindicated one would expect 'a) the absence of high valuation ratios, and b) the predominance of low valuation ratios.'‡ He found a wide range of valuation ratios among his seventy-four takeovers and concluded that neither requirement a) nor b) above held. His results for valuation ratios relative to the bidding firms, and industry averages showed little difference between victim firms in terms of the proportions occupying three groups of valuation ratios, $0.0 - 1.0$, $1.0 - 2.0$, and 2.0 and over.§

It is interesting to note the differing conclusions both authors reached with regard to the failure of the valuation ratio to emerge as an important determinant to takeover activity. Newbould suggests that the inability of the valuation ratio to offer any explanation of the incidence of mergers and in particular to indicate those firms which receive bids, is perhaps '. . . another example of the excess rationality imputed by economists into the actions of management.'¶ He instead opts for an *ad hoc* questionnaire approach to discover the managerial motivations behind mergers. Singh on the other hand attempted to place his results in the context of the new theories of the firm (e.g. Baumol (1959), Marris (1964), and Williamson (1964)) and the stock market as a control mechanism on managerial actions. In finding only a weak inverse relationship between the valuation ratio and profitability and the likeli-

---

* There is nothing in the theory which suggests that raiders' valuation ratios should be greater than those of the firms they acquire, only that the acquired firm be undervalued relative to what the raider could earn with its assets. As an approximation to this one can relate the acquired firm's valuation to the industry average valuation, or treat the relationship as a probability function as done in this study.

† Industry averages were constructed from a sample of reports immediately prior to the offer. Since the averages sometimes contained as few as six firms, this rough measure presents a likely source of bias.

‡ Newbould (1970), p. 99.

§ It is not possible to comment on the significance of Newbould's proportions since no significance tests were undertaken.

¶ Newbould (1970), p. 107.

hood of takeover, but a marginally clearer result for size he concluded that with qualification,* this provided positive support for the new theories of the firm. A strong control mechanism would on the other hand have lent support to the neo-classical theory of the firm since whatever their intentions, management would be constrained to maximise profits by the desire for survival; the failure to do so would result in being taken over. His results for profitability and size suggest support for the new theories since these theories have variables in their objective functions related to size (e.g. salary power, prestige) or aspects of size (e.g. growth, sales revenue, or the volume of slack) and whose achievement involves the sacrifice of profits. Thus managers are not constrained to pursue profits since they can reduce the threat of takeover by becoming larger, '. . . the fear of takeover, rather than being a constraint on managerial discretion may also encourage them in the same direction.'†

While the results contained in this study are not identical to Singh's, (i.e. the valuation ratio seems to play a significant role in the majority of industries in the takeover process while there was little indication that size affected the firm's likelihood of takeover), one is loath to interpret the results at this stage of the analysis in terms of the appropriate theoretical model of the theory of the firm. A common characteristic of the new theories is the existence of some form of constraint on managerial discretion which prevents managers from totally sacrificing profits to the achievement of their posited objective. Central to Marris's theory formulated in the UK climate where takeovers are extremely common is the notion that the constraint becomes operational through the inverse relationship between the valuation ratio and the threat of takeover. This is because managers have a desire for security which is therefore competing with the primary ingredient in their objective function. The sacrifice of profits to the objective of growth is constrained because of the effect the low profits (and the levels of the other decision variables chosen to maximise growth) have on the valuation ratio and hence the likelihood of

* Singh (1971), p. 145.
† Singh (1971), p. 144.

takeover. Hence, the existence of some sort of constraint either through profits or as in Marris's theory as a result of a desire for security from the danger of takeover, prevents managers from pursuing unrestricted and unprofitable growth. The existence of an inverse valuation ratio takeover relationship is therefore a necessary condition of this theory as formulated. It is however by no means sufficient, because one would also expect a profit maximising firm to choose takeover candidates on the basis of expected profitability on the purchase price of the investment and hence *ceteris paribus* choose the firm with lowest valuation ratio.

As Singh, among others,* has noted, only if the relationship were perfect would the new theories be invalidated. An imperfect but real relationship as contained in the results of this study only satisfies a necessary condition of the Marris hypothesis but does not give any guide to the appropriate motivational scheme to impute to managers; whether profit maximisation, growth maximisation or something else. However in view of the very minor role played by the valuation ratio contained in Singh's results, it would seem to contradict the necessary condition embodied in Marris's new theory rather than support such revisions simply because size appears marginally to increase security (i.e. since size is related to the objective) and the sacrifice of profits does not seem to reduce security (i.e. they can pursue their objective semi-independently of profits). Of course, constraints can be imposed from directions other than the fear of takeover. For example, loss of job through dismissal by owners or bankruptcy resulting from the excessive sacrifice of profits or limitations on growth imposed through the supply of managerial expertise† could provide the requisite constraints on the managerial objectives. What is important to note is that neither these results nor Singh's yield any clues to the nature and appropriateness of the posited objectives of the new theories of the firm. The difference lies in the fact that

---

* See Markham (1955).
† This suggestion is fully developed in Penrose (1959). One should note however that this source of constraint on the managerial objective may be weak where growth is achieved through takeovers, as the raider is in a sense purchasing a supply of managerial expertise along with the assets of the firm.

those contained here seem to support a necessary condition for the acceptance of the Marris model while Singh's suggest the requisite constraints on managerial discretion must lie elsewhere and hence is in direct opposition to Marris's thesis.

A third interpretation of the survival of unprofitable and undervalued firms is offered by Brian Hindley* in a critical analysis of the results of D. C. Mueller† where the latter suggests growth maximisation as a motive behind mergers. The evidence of the survival of inefficient firms however is seen by Hindley as evidence against both growth maximisation and present value maximisation hypotheses. He bases this on the view that growth maximisers should be more eager to acquire under-valued firms (i.e. ones with low valuation ratios) than present value maximisers so that presumably for undervalued firms to survive suggests neither objective is commonly encountered in the population of firms. While admitting that some of the survivors may be owner controlled and hence able to block an unwanted offer or that a less dramatic control change could have occurred, he simply asserts‡ these explanations have not been sufficient to explain all the survivors.§ He concludes therefore that, 'Demonstration of an inefficient takeover system would therefore be a major step towards rejecting growth maximising models in favour of some form of non-aggressive 'easy-life' managerial model of the firm.'¶ My arguments in this study make further comment on his inter-pretation unnecessary. If refutation or otherwise of the growth maximisation hypothesis rests solely on defining at what level the takeover mechanism is agreed to be inefficient, the theory is unlikely ever to get much support.

I shall not however leave the discussion of the relevance of takeovers to the new theories of the firm in this rather un-satisfactory state. In the next chapter I shall look at takeovers

* Hindley (1972).
† Mueller (1969).
‡ Hindley (1969).
§ On this point, see Kuehn and Davies (1973) in which owner control (a variable available only in the last few years) serves to explain the survival of the majority of poor performers (performance measured both in terms of profitability and valuation ratio).
¶ Hindley (1972).

in terms of the factors which directly affect the valuation ratio, these being the financial characteristics of the firm which are, in part, determined by managers' decisions. It is hoped that by doing so, some indication of the nature of the typical taken over firm will be revealed and that this will shed further light on the nature of the takeover mechanism as a constraint on managerial discretion. Then in chapter 5 I shall employ an alternative estimational technique, that of probit analysis, in the investigation of the nature of the takeover process and its role as a constraint on managerial discretion. Finally, in chapter 6, I shall attempt to consider directly the relevance of the growth maximising hypothesis whereby takeovers will be regarded as not only a constraint on the growth objective but also a vehicle for its achievement. By attempting to derive predictions for the growth maximising hypothesis for raiders which are mutually exclusive to predictions from the assumption that raiders are profit maximisers, it may be possible to test the relevance of the theory in terms of its posited objective rather than simply finding that a necessary condition for its acceptance has been satisfied. By doing so it is hoped that some evidence will be provided on which a choice can be made between the two behavioral positions. In doing so, I will be attempting to accomplish the third aim of this study: to relate takeovers to the new theories of the firm.

4 Linear Probability Models of Takeovers II:

Industry Analysis of the Firm's Financial Characteristics

4.1 INTRODUCTION

In this chapter I shall attempt to capture the influence the firm's financial characteristics – profit rate, growth rate, retention ratio, and liquidity ratio – have on whether or not the firm is taken over. As in model I, the relationship will be estimated at the industry level by means of the linear probability function technique. The purpose is not only to discover whether there are significant differences in the performance of taken over and surviving firms, but also to investigate the effect of some of the variables which might be expected to influence the basic valuation ratio takeover relationship explored in the previous chapter.

4.2 THE MODEL

In chapter 2 was discussed the likely influence the four variables to be employed would have on the probability that a firm is taken over. It was anticipated that the average acquired firm would be less profitable, have grown more slowly, tend to retain a greater proportion of after tax profits, and be more liquid than the average surviving firm. Regressions are undertaken for each of the sixty-six industries in order to remove the 'noise' attributable to large inter-industry variations in the levels of performance. As before, however, some comment will be possible regarding industry differences in the strength and character of the takeover – financial variable relationship based upon the regression results.

For each industry, six regressions were run based upon various formulations of the four financial variables* included in each equation. The dependent variable is a dummy taking the value of 0 if the firm survived and 1 if it was taken over. All four variables were averaged over the available years if the firm survived. If it was taken over, the profit rate, retention ratio and liquidity ratio were measured as either the annual level in the latest accounting period prior to the offer, or the average of the two years prior to the offer, and finally as the average of the three years prior to the offer, while the growth rate was measured as the average level over the three years preceding the offer. As before, the above variables were also related to the industry average for the relevant year(s) if the firm was taken over and the average for all years if it survived. For all variables the relationship is assumed to be linear in the estimation process.

The definitions of the variables to be employed appear below:

T = a dummy variable taking the value 1 if the firm was taken over and 0 if it was not.

if $T = 0$ then

P_0 = the before tax profit rate of the firm averaged over all available years

P_0/PA_0 = P_0 divided by the average before tax profit rate of all firms in the industry averaged over all available years

G_0 = the firm's growth rate of net assets over all available years

G_0/GA_0 = G_0 divided by the average of all firm's growth rates over the period

R_0 = the retention ratio of the firm averaged over all available years

R_0/RA_0 = R_0 divided by the average retention ratio of all firms in the industry averaged over all available years

L_0 = the liquidity ratio of the firm averaged over all available years

---

* The definitions of these variables appear in appendix I section II.G

$L_0/LA_0 = L_0$ divided by the average liquidity ratio of all firms in the industry averaged over all available years

if $T = 1$ then

$P_1 =$ the before tax profit rate of the firm at the accounting period prior to the offer

$P_2 =$ the before tax profit rate of the firm averaged over the two accounting periods prior to the offer

$P_3 =$ the before tax profit rate of the firm averaged over the three accounting periods prior to the offer

$P_1/PA_1 = P_1$ divided by the average before tax protfi rate of all firms in the industry for the year in which P_1 was measured

$P_2/PA_2 = P_2$ divided by the average before tax profit rate of all firms in the industry for the two years in which P_2 was measured

$P_3/PA_3 = P_3$ divided by the average before tax profit rate of all firms in the industry for the three years in which P_3 was measured

$G_1 =$ the firm's growth rate of net assets over the three years prior to the offer

$G_1/GA_1 = G_1$ divided by the growth rate of net assets of all firms in the industry over the three years in which G_1 was measured

$R_1 =$ the retention ratio of the firm at the accounting period prior to the offer

$R_2 =$ the retention ratio of the firm averaged over the two accounting periods prior to the offer

$R_3 =$ the retention ratio of the firm averaged over the three accounting periods prior to the offer

$R_1/RA_1 = R_1$ divided by the average retention ratio of all firms in the industry for the year in which R_1 was measured

$R_2/RA_2 = R_2$ divided by the average retention ratio of all firms in the industry for the two years in which R_2 was measured

$R_3/RA_3 = R_3$ divided by the average retention ratio of all firms in the industry for the three years in which R_3 was measured

L_1 = the liquidity ratio of the firm at the accounting period prior to the offer

L_2 = the liquidity ratio of the firm averaged over the two accounting periods prior to the offer

L_3 = the liquidity ratio of the firm averaged over the three accounting periods prior to the offer

L_1/LA_1 = L_1 divided by the average liquidity ratio of all firms in the industry for the year in which L_1 was measured

L_2/LA_2 = L_2 divided by the average liquidity ratio of all firms in the industry for the two years in which L_2 was measured

L_3/LA_3 = L_3 divided by the average liquidity ratio of all firms in the industry for the three years in which L_3 was measured

Using these variables, the following six regression equations were derived, each employing comparable measures of the four independent variables:

1) if $T = 0$: P_0, G_0, R_0, L_0; if $T = 1$: P_1, G_1, R_1, L_1
2) if $T = 0$: P_0, G_0, R_0, L_0; if $T = 1$: P_2, G_1, R_2, L_2
3) if $T = 0$: P_0, G_0, R_0, L_0; if $T = 1$: P_3, G_1, R_3, L_3
4) if $T = 0$: P_0/PA_0, G_0/GA_0, R_0/RA_0, L_0/LA_0
   if $T = 1$: P_1/PA_1, G_1/GA_1, R_1/RA_1, L_1/LA_1
5) if $T = 0$: P_0/PA_0, G_0/GA_0, R_0/RA_0, L_0/LA_0
   if $T = 1$: P_2/PA_2, G_1/GA_1, R_2/RA_2, L_2/LA_2
6) if $T = 0$: P_0/PA_0, G_0/GA_0, R_0/RA_0, L_0/LA_0
   if $T = 1$: P_3/PA_3, G_1/GA_1, R_3/RA_3, L_3/LA_3

4.3 RESULTS

A sample of the results appear in tables 4.1 and 4.2 and a summary of the results for all industries is contained in table 4.3 below. Table 4.1 gives the complete results again for the furnishing industry, selected purely for illustration. Table 4.2 presents two regression results for each industry, one selected from regressions 1 to 3 and the second from regressions 4 to 6. They were chosen on the basis of being the equations which most clearly demonstrate the total effect of the financial variables on the probability of takeover. An interpretation of these results and conclusions are contained in section 4.4

TABLE 4.1

Regressions on the Furnishing Industry Dummy Dependent Variable on the Firm's Financial Variables

Regression	Constant	Profit Rate	Growth Rate	Retention Ratio	Liquidity Ratio	F	$\bar{R}^2$
1	0·49952 (0·08801)	−0·69500 (0·34156)	−0·60836 (0·21055)	0·00093* (0·11498)	−0·25846* (0·21268)	4·66547	0·10702
2	0·51987 (0·08796)	−0·74495 (0·36451)	−0·61021 (0·12419)	−0·04964* (0·12419)	−0·33861* (0·21254)	5·09347	0·11883
3	0·47759 (0·09232)	−0·71821 (0·35904)	−0·62406 (0·20906)	0·03655* (0·12491)	−0·35887* (0·20896)	5·17025	0·12092
4	0·33971 (0·06819)	−0·14494 (0·05457)	−0·00207* (0·02227)	−0·02267* (0·03257)	0·01966 (0·00625)	5·31036	0·12865
5	0·25268 (0·07721)	−0·13566 (0·05398)	−0·00208* (0·02254)	−0·00894* (0·04950)	0·03534* (0·01904)	2·73786	0·05316
6	0·15945 (0·07635)	−0·11816 (0·05248)	−0·00541* (0·02248)	0·03608 (0·04524)	0·03994 (0·01988)	2·88873	0·05929

Note: standard errors of the associated parameter estimates appear below each in brackets. Also, only those parameter estimates marked with an asterisk (*) fail to emerge as significant at the 5 per cent level.

TABLE 4.2

Selected Regression Results: All Industries – Financial Variables

Industry	Regression	Constant	Profit Rate	Growth Rate	Retention Ratio	Liquidity Ratio	F	$\bar{R}^2$
1	1	0·44295	-0·82366*	-0·14087	0·15589*	0·06574*	2·80459	0·07049
	5	0·30553	-0·19047	-0·00753*	0·11886	-0·02696*	3·56424	0·08449
2	3	0·46926	-0·05328*	-0·73847	0·17585*	0·45360*	3·06583	0·05941
	4	0·29743	-0·05112*	-0·15862	-0·07776*	-0·00674	4·46148	0·10127
3	3	0·48559	0·43979*	-0·03699*	-0·21892*	0·45961*	0·55630*	-0·06419
	5	-0·00220*	0·22613*	-0·01469*	0·09695*	0·01713	1·70551*	0·03810
4	1	0·69063	-1·83605	0·01052*	-0·11517*	-0·30115*	5·16189	0·10893
	6	0·44981	-0·21939	0·00865*	-0·08212*	0·02125	4·91419	0·10804
5	1	0·31231	-0·15034*	-0·02002*	-0·00801*	0·24412*	1·99676*	0·01650
	4	0·17417	-0·21783*	0·00010*	-0·00270*	-0·03047*	1·04530*	-0·00467
6	3	0·50569	0·04495*	-0·52822	-0·00308*	0·13387	6·91547	0·09114
	5	0·31658	0·00881*	-0·03956*	-0·00007*	-0·03329*	2·02595*	0·01373
7	3	0·45931	0·26474*	-1·51487	0·26849*	0·15654*	4·50062	0·13404
	6	0·28161	0·01645*	-0·03080*	-0·06264*	0·00095	2·64946	0·07033
8	1	0·46162	-0·83018	-0·01229*	-0·00834*	-0·34491	4·23576	0·06034
	5	0·12768	-0·00027*	-0·00537	-0·00227*	0·00895	4·10944	0·05852
9	1	0·45289	-0·39730*	-0·03933*	0·02910*	-0·22398*	4·19196	0·04020
	5	0·25158	-0·07833*	-0·00219*	0·06629	0·00860	4·14449	0·04069

10	2	0·37741	−0·18706*	0·03327*	0·17976	−0·15383*	2·96375	0·02066
	6	0·11567	0·00402*	−0·00221*	−0·00250*	0·00249	3·56792	0·02816
11	1	0·51286	−1·29796	−0·36843	0·11849*	−0·22140*	5·57998	0·10776
	4	0·26537	−0·17167	0·00811*	0·08686	0·00014*	3·39063	0·05882
12	1	0·53950	−0·90567	−0·20521	−0·00087*	−0·02301*	5·79040	0·06773
	4	0·38035	−0·20457	−0·07052	−0·00058*	−0·00312*	5·49149	0·06476
13	2	−0·07672*	1·15024*	−0·31300*	0·18437	−0·09913	2·45736*	0·12438
	5	0·12912*	−0·04389*	0·08450*	0·04838	0·00562*	1·77060*	0·05936
14	2	0·40918	0·00494*	−0·30537	−0·00219*	−0·14922*	3·00748	0·03623
	5	0·22427	−0·00230*	−0·00914*	−0·00088*	−0·01081*	0·91593*	−0·00744
15	1	0·45832	−0·90381	−0·03173*	−0·03860*	0·30363*	1·72627*	0·01392
	6	0·21774	−0·07781*	−0·00082*	−0·01250*	0·00106	1·92442*	0·02033
16	1	0·58542	−0·84531	−0·09222	−0·01930*	−0·10486*	4·53753	0·05134
	5	0·45097	−0·18418	−0·00258*	−0·00343*	−0·00078*	3·13163	0·03116
17	2	0·52976	−0·50697*	−0·30148	−0·00998*	−0·07670*	4·16579	0·03683
	4	0·31383	−0·09957	0·02287*	−0·00339*	0·00067*	1·49716*	0·00332
18	1	0·20766*	0·48607*	−0·18663*	0·35614*	0·17092*	1·24511*	−0·00059
	4	0·28388	−0·11318*	0·04147*	0·03070*	0·00853	2·05577*	0·08898
19	3	0·60244	0·26259*	−1·45197	−0·25704*	−0·08066*	1·65400*	0·03467
	5	0·37298	−0·13643*	0·00710*	−0·03396*	−0·01229*	0·68694*	−0·05527
20	2	0·55800	−1·47427	−0·16400*	−0·00276*	−0·31094*	3·78468	0·11374
	4	0·39002	−0·17264	0·00457*	−0·04312*	−0·00748*	2·57142	0·06271
21	2	0·56319	0·40056*	−0·67500*	−0·12654*	−0·03791*	1·06997*	−0·01215
	4	0·20367*	0·07449*	0·09964*	0·09597	−0·01625*	3·46190	0·13040

TABLE 4.2 – cont.

Selected Regression Results: All Industries – Financial Variables

Industry	Regression	Constant	Profit Rate	Growth Rate	Retention Ratio	Liquidity Ratio	F	$\bar{R}^2$
22	3	0·47759	−0·71821	−0·62406	0·03655*	−0·35887*	5·17025	0·12092
	4	0·33971	−0·14494	−0·00207*	−0·02267*	0·01966	5·31036	0·12865
23	2	0·44761	−0·60786*	−0·05075*	−0·00211*	0·18799*	1·58664*	−0·00933
	4	0·29022	−0·08518*	−0·00251*	−0·00026*	0·02309	1·52947*	−0·00787
24	2	0·40517	−0·64795*	−0·52042*	0·50366*	0·75148*	2·37020*	0·09640
	6	0·56840	−0·12026*	−0·00451*	−0·11528*	−0·03048*	0·86082*	−0·04158
25	1	0·60951	−0·66903	−0·23331	−0·05808*	−0·15399*	4·85132	0·06225
	4	0·49450	−0·16312	−0·00055*	−0·03412*	0·00006*	3·22728	0·03597
26	2	0·53827	−1·54688	0·00042*	0·07021*	0·23567*	3·20877	0·05854
	4	0·17857	−0·08716*	−0·00068*	0·08614	−0·03343*	3·65751	0·07207
27	2	0·53984	−1·08908*	−0·13631*	−0·01558*	0·17612*	1·59973*	0·02437
	4	0·20426	−0·11718*	−0·02250*	0·08418	0·00401*	3·68028	0·15020
28	1	0·59174	−0·56042*	−0·22098*	0·04621*	0·06756*	1·50770*	0·01272
	6	0·34730	0·02495*	−0·01557*	−0·09884*	0·01819*	1·10234*	−0·00805
29	1	0·37507	−0·20454*	−0·14650*	0·00120*	−0·25343*	1·02631*	−0·00657
	6	0·22221	−0·05534*	0·02840*	−0·00750*	0·04479	5·72477	0·12185
30	3	0·37701	−0·10571*	−0·06574*	0·19540*	0·30552*	1·45994*	0·00673
	5	0·38772	−0·13350	0·00090*	0·04925*	−0·03507*	1·72879*	0·01611

31	1	0.41726	1.02658*	−0.77760	−0.16556*	−0.87663*	1.99115*	0.05597
	6	0.24718*	0.05299*	0.01339*	−0.12104*	0.03116	2.31210*	0.08131
32	3	0.49612	−0.26205*	−0.36706*	−0.13500*	0.17977*	0.64728*	−0.05175
	4	0.24409	−0.05474*	−0.00338*	−0.02636*	0.00983	1.15430*	−0.00787
33	2	0.56599	−1.39140	0.10623*	0.07803*	0.23703*	2.87950	0.13434
	5	0.48262	−0.29142	0.07252*	−0.03837*	0.04146	4.50393	0.24096
34	3	0.63482	−1.14622	−0.21344*	0.01982*	0.08576*	3.98823	0.09784
	6	0.39409	−0.13201*	−0.00094*	−0.03384*	−0.03339*	1.68352*	0.01850
35	2	0.58941	−0.65885*	−0.44132	0.11063*	0.22560*	2.03287*	0.04282
	4	0.49288	−0.13236*	−0.01818*	0.02339*	−0.00122*	1.13372*	−0.00679
36	1	0.95059	−1.09266*	−0.11322*	−0.39468*	−0.49298*	4.26752	0.06817
	5	0.80793	−0.19816	−0.00723*	−0.09785*	−0.00810*	2.91828	0.04102
37	2	0.58909	−1.86075	0.10329*	0.04585*	0.07100*	3.90494	0.14232
	5	0.30945	−0.21307	0.05817*	0.05641*	0.03679	5.84883	0.22326
38	1	0.62708	−0.67870	−0.12923*	−0.05576*	0.10577*	4.43903	0.06652
	5	0.39921	−0.08397*	−0.00460*	−0.02510*	0.00061*	1.84482*	0.01334
39	1	0.59732	−0.70900*	−0.13489*	−0.10508*	−0.08175*	2.31689*	0.03942
	5	0.52717	−0.18510	−0.00927*	−0.04543*	0.00851	3.45489	0.08180
40	1	0.60564	−0.12840*	−0.12513*	0.38085	−0.16474*	2.76784	0.07678
	6	0.58000	−0.20290*	−0.05927*	−0.17231	0.11978*	3.63992	0.12016
41	2	0.66686	−0.47011*	−0.06205*	−0.02918*	0.15668*	3.18498	0.02957
	4	0.55013	−0.12057*	0.00003*	−0.00115*	−0.00810*	2.11280*	0.01378
42	3	0.39143	0.44053	−0.15908	0.21527*	0.35440*	5.18205	0.15163
	6	0.15732	0.09934	−0.07039	0.16640	0.00013*	2.08009*	0.03938

TABLE 4.2 – cont.

Selected Regression Results: All Industries – Financial Variables

Industry	Regression	Constant	Profit Rate	Growth Rate	Retention Ratio	Liquidity Ratio	F	$\bar{R}^2$
43	3	0·72826	0·78171*	-1·39705	-0·48028*	-0·61159*	5·89940	0·27512
	4	0·09913*	-0·05436*	-0·11302*	0·13973*	0·02444*	2·19320*	0·07431
44	3	0·73951	-0·33375*	-0·79726	0·15288*	-0·58441*	2·38836*	0·08197
	5	0·42935*	-0·07969*	-0·04586*	0·15569*	0·00044*	-0·67665*	-0·05130
45	2	0·74091	-0·24442*	-0·16987*	0·69909	-0·23381*	1·90596*	0·05751
	5	0·46291	-0·01461*	-0·01381*	-0·18360*	-0·03504*	1·27813*	0·00274
46	2	0·48496	-0·94991*	-0·09090*	-0·10362*	-0·17418*	1·65224*	0·01972
	6	0·32147	-0·13771*	-0·00351*	-0·01066*	-0·00352*	1·16915*	-0·00451
47	3	0·56589	-0·42121*	-0·16312	-0·08746*	-0·22092	3·20763	-0·05090
	5	0·35040	-0·05358*	-0·01870*	-0·05530*	-0·00027*	1·13602*	-0·00324
48	3	0·81080	-0·95503	-0·26979	-0·06016*	0·18756*	3·52894	0·10968
	4	0·49658	-0·16025*	-0·01962*	0·10982*	-0·00180*	1·93977*	0·03691
49	2	0·77880	-1·19026	-0·24539*	-0·21198*	0·25882*	2·95879	0·08153
	6	0·33270	-0·10821*	-0·10099*	-0·05427*	-0·05645	2·28815	0·05919
50	1	0·76212	-0·89268*	-0·18938	-0·21838*	-0·16330*	2·77107	0·06332
	6	0·31327	-0·08458*	-0·00572*	0·10616*	0·08104	2·17031*	0·04679

51	2	0·77782	−1·29890	−0·48282	0·37264	−0·26348*	4·97837	0·14491
	5	0·49067	−0·11210*	−0·00666*	0·12439	0·00349*	2·21664*	0·04556
52	1	0·45497	−1·57757	−0·09662*	0·31369*	0·67311*	4·20212	0·23708
	4	0·22148	−0·24738	0·00315*	0·18178	−0·00732*	4·58830	0·26003
53	1	0·63371	−1·23843	0·16028*	−0·02277*	0·31138*	2·21207*	0·03441
	4	0·41543	−0·08924*	0·00352*	0·00507	−0·00440*	2·76938	0·05423
54	2	0·65693	−1·29686	−0·07111*	−0·02219*	0·32019*	5·02213	0·06473
	4	0·53422	−0·19245	0·00026*	−0·00063*	0·01169	6·85447	0·09687
55	2	0·58904	−0·08477*	−0·26832	−0·06846*	−0·43511*	2·15565*	0·03788
	5	0·37619	0·02507*	−0·01526*	−0·02407*	0·01866*	0·54139*	−0·03252
56	1	0·56969	−0·82155	−0·11168*	−0·05174*	0·28781*	3·36638	−0·05942
	4	0·37099	−0·11870	0·02039*	−0·01475*	0·00574*	2·46836	0·00930
57	1	0·63202	−1·08172	−0·42403	−0·03991*	0·24761*	6·29222	0·13612
	5	0·37322	−0·09013*	−0·03720*	−0·01787*	0·00227	4·54294	0·09891
58	1	0·60155	0·86078*	−1·89850	−0·29880*	−0·17332*	3·05324	0·23109
	6	0·53237	0·05882*	−0·04122*	−0·35040*	−0·06732*	1·51234*	0·04553
59	1	0·54555	−0·15788*	0·18565	−0·14984*	−0·06283*	3·98833	0·11658
	5	0·21503	−0·03229*	−0·02682*	−0·00532*	0·01267	1·71400*	0·07130
61	2	0·56079	−1·33212	−0·04296	−0·03795*	0·12680*	5·07489	0·05639
	5	0·46751	−0·12232	−0·00977*	0·06925	0·00096*	4·88924	0·05482
62	1	0·52483	−1·16741	−0·15329*	0·14532*	−0·14195*	4·46199	0·10810
	6	0·29508	−0·11123*	−0·00318*	−0·00105*	0·00184	1·95364*	0·02764
63	3	0·28703*	0·94678*	−0·80527	0·28448*	−0·41559*	1·09305*	−0·01881
	4	0·10568*	0·13310*	−0·06275*	0·06242	−0·00125*	1·62876*	0·04266

Table 4.2 – cont.

Selected Regression Results: All Industries – Financial Variables

Industry	Regression	Constant	Profit Rate	Growth Rate	Retention Ratio	Liquidity Ratio	F	$\bar{R}^2$
64	3	0·31805*	1·43854*	−0·57710*	−0·16486*	−0·05710*	0·58755*	−0·07714
	4	0·48331	−0·19774*	0·02847*	−0·07770*	0·00285*	0·40057*	−0·10422
65	3	0·19768	1·06188*	−0·56975	0·22261	−0·03325*	2·93716	0·08909
	4	0·15813	0·06749*	−0·04412*	0·06175*	0·02369	2·89579	0·08710
66	1	0·51533	0·92465*	−0·59542*	0·32913	−0·40605*	1·41778	0·01502
	5	0·43764	0·02364*	−0·03016*	−0·14861*	0·00236	1·64703*	0·03562
67	1	0·66709	−0·62880*	−0·19621*	−0·26295*	0·01002*	1·48076*	0·02102
	4	0·56256	−0·20666*	0·07271*	−0·19569*	0·00609*	1·93160*	0·06235

Note: parameter estimates and F statistics marked with an asterisk (*) fail to emerge as significant at the 5 per cent level.

TABLE 4.3

Financial Characteristics Regressions – Summary

Regression no.	No. of industries with significant correct signs				Proportion of industries with significant correct signs (%)			
	P–R	G–R	R–R	L–R	P–R	G–R	R–R	L–R
1	22	26	3	2	33·3	39·4	4·6	3·0
2	20	24	6	4	30·3	36·4	9·1	6·1
3	14	27	4	1	21·2	40·9	6·1	1·5
4	22	4	9	9	33·3	6·1	13·6	13·6
5	19	3	10	13	28·8	4·6	15·2	19·7
6	12	3	7	18	18·2	4·6	10·6	27·3

4.4   INTERPRETATION OF RESULTS AND CONCLUSIONS

I shall initially discuss in this section the interpretation of the regression results for the furnishing industry (table 4.1) which will serve as an introduction and guide to an analysis of the results of two regressions for each industry contained in table 4.2. I shall then comment upon the summary of results for all regressions undertaken in all industries appearing in table 4.3 and attempt to provide an explanation for the differing industry results with an industry characteristic analysis similar to that contained in section 3.4 of the previous chapter. Finally, I shall comment upon these results and how they might relate to the theory of the firm.

It can readily be seen that the results for the furnishing industry are in accordance with the interpretation of the regression equations as linear probability functions. In all six regressions in table 4.1 the intercept is positive and less than 1. Since all parameter estimates which are significantly different from zero (except liquidity in regressions 4 to 6) are negative, the predicted value of the probability of takeover will never exceed 1. Thus the probability that a firm will get taken over is inversely related to both its profit rate and growth rate, although the effect of the latter disappears (though still retaining the theoretically anticipated negative sign) when the growth rate is taken as relative to the appropriate industry average. In this industry the retention policy and hence dividend policy made no apparent impact on whether or not the firm was taken over. With liquidity in regressions 4 to 6, it should be pointed out that for the vast majority of firms and for all industries, the average liquidity ratio is negative. A negative sign for the parameter estimate for regressions 1 to 3 will imply that the less liquid a firm becomes (i.e. the ratio becomes more negative), the greater is its chance of being taken over. For regressions 4 to 6, a positive sign for the parameter estimate will imply the same thing since the value for each firm is being divided by the (negative) industry average. In terms of the interpretation of the equation as a probability function, it remains possible for the predicted value to take on values of greater than 1 if the firm is extremely burdened by debt (i.e. highly illiquid) and the industry average liquidity is negative and very small in absolute value. In general, this possibility is precluded by the size of the parameter estimate, it normally being very small in absolute value in regressions 4 to 6. For example, in regression 6 for the furnishing industry, even if the profit rate (the only other significant variable) were 0 it would require that the firm be more than 28 times less liquid than the industry average before the conditional probability of takeover exceeded unity. Similarly, for regression 4, where liquidity is also significant, the firm would have to be more than 35 times less liquid than the industry average before the probability exceeded unity and the interpretation of the predicted values as conditional probabilities were to break down.

Returning to the first three regressions where the profit rate and growth rate are significant, it can be seen that increasing both will reduce the predicted probability of takeover. If both are zero, the firm has approximately a 50 per cent chance of being taken over on the basis of the estimated value of the intercept. Because of the recognised correlation between profits and growth, they will, in general, both tend to move together as they influence the probability of takeover. The empirical correlation is by no means perfect, however, for as Marris has argued,* high rates of growth may involve the sacrifice of profits so that the two can be inversely related.

* See the previous discussion on this point in section 2.5 page 51 and the related footnote.

To the extent that this trade-off between growth and profitability occurs, one can interpret regressions 1 to 3 as indicating the choice of high growth and low profits or low growth and high profits as a means of reducing the probability of takeover and providing security. For instance, the same level of security could be achieved by earning an average of 15 per cent return on net assets but growing at an average rate of 65 per cent per year as one could achieve by growing at 20 per cent per year but earning 55 per cent return on net assets as both reduce the predicted probability of takeover to zero.* Slightly more reasonable levels of performance can be related to some positive but acceptable chance of takeover in the same way.

The above interpretation is not however strictly correct in so far as there is a large residual variance to the estimated equations. If however this variation is attributable to either unknown or unalterable characteristics of the firm (such as the industry class or dispersion of shareholding) then perhaps the above calculations would take on more significance. That is, if management wished to avoid being taken over, they would only be expected to take appropriate actions on the variables they can influence – profits, growth, retentions and liquidity.† This is precisely why the equations were specified in the way they were (and why no additional variables were added in order to attempt to improve the R^2 value).‡ Furthermore, if a choice is available between growth and profitability to achieve the desired level of security as is apparently the case in the furnishing industry, managers may operate primarily on one of the variables, ensuring the other remained at a satisfactory level – the desired level of security possibly involving a trade-off between the costs (difficulties) of reducing the probability of takeover to zero and the acceptance of some small but positive threat of takeover. In fact, Marris has argued that

---

* These calculations refer to the relationship estimated in regression 1.

† A potentially important omitted discretionary variable is gearing, but data were not available for this. In any case, Singh found it not to be an important discriminator of the acquired and surviving firms.

‡ For example, one could have added the age of the company which was found in section 1.5 pp. 31–2, to be related to the probability of takeover but this obviously is in no sense a discretionary variable at managers' disposal.

the managers would choose to maximise growth subject to a profits constraint (which operates through the valuation ratio) for reasons mentioned previously as the method for achieving satisfactory levels of security.

With the bulk of the industries, however, profits and growth do not both emerge as significant. Taking regression 1, there are only 8 industries for which the parameter estimates for both profits and growth are significant, while there are 32 additional industries for which either is significant. A likely explanation for this is that the inter-correlation between the two explanatory variables, resulting in multicollinearity, makes it very difficult, if not impossible, to disentangle their separate influences and obtain reasonably precise estimates of their relative effects. The impact of the joint effect of profitability and growth on the probability of takeover emerges in either one or the other of the two explanatory variables.

Thus, if it were possible to break the correlation between profitability and growth one could get at the separate effects of each in the estimated equation. If one estimated the relationship with profits and growth separately one would be likely to find that both were significantly even within some of the 18 industries for which neither were significant. I shall, in the next chapter, be able to shed some light on this problem when the financial variables appear separately in the relationships estimated by means of the probit transformation.

Looking at table 4.2 in more detail, it can be seen that regressions 1 and 4 usually provide the best form of the relationship, these being the equations corresponding to the employment of the latest pre-bid data for the taken over firms. In the first set, regressions 1 to 3, the breakdown is as follows: regression 1 appears in table 4.2 for 28 industries, regression 2 in 21 industries and regression 3 in 17 industries. In the second set where the variables are related to the industry average, regression 4 appears for 26 industries, regression 5 for 24 industries and regression 6 for 16 industries. It would appear from this that the performance of the firm immediately prior to the bid, whether in absolute terms or relative to the industry performance in that year, more often offers the best indicator of whether or not the firm is taken over.* This impression is

* With the qualification that in some cases these equations are not significant

confirmed by the profits variable in table 4.3 where in one-third of the industries it emerges as significant in regression 1 but declines to just over one-fifth in regression 3. An even more dramatic decline is noticeable between regression 4 and regression 6.

It can also be noticed that the regression equations in table 4.2 can be sensibly interpreted as linear probability functions as was illustrated with the furnishing industry. In all but 11 of the 132 regressions in table 4.2 the intercept is significant, positive and less than unity. Furthermore, the significant parameter estimates with the exception of liquidity take on the theoretically anticipated sign. Increases in both profits and growth will reduce the chance of takeover.

The effect of retentions are, however, weak as can be seen from table 4.2. At best only in 6 industries does the retention ratio emerge as a significant influence on the probability of takeover although in each case it takes on the correct sign such that high retention ratios are associated with a high risk of takeover. This is marginally improved upon in the second set where the retention ratio is measured relative to the industry average. We noted in section 1.5 the possibility that the retention ratio has its effect on the probability of takeover by way of a U-shaped relationship. This speculation emerged from an inspection of table 1.8c which contains the proportions of acquired firms to the total within various groups of the retention ratio. What appears to be happening is that any effect of retentions is being obscured by extreme values at both ends of the scale. On the one hand, negative values of retentions can only occur when profits are so low that required dividend payments (i.e. on preference shares), result in exceeding the after tax level of profits and results in the ratio becoming negative. On the other hand, it is not possible by definition to retain greater than 100 per cent of after tax earnings. Values of the ratio greater than 1 occurring in table 1.8c therefore result from the firm making losses and paying out some required level of dividends exceeding the value of the losses. In this case, the ratio would result in positive values greater than 1. However, both these extreme values correspond to the same argument concerning the role of retentions: that the retention ratio for firms earning low profits or making losses is not a discretionary variable and its level is determined by the necessity of servicing the preferred equity. Thus these companies would face a high risk of takeover not because of either very high or negative values of the retention ratio, but because of their poor profit position. Negative values would serve to obscure the anticipated effect that high retentions are associated with a high threat of takeover when retentions act as a discretionary variable affecting the valuation ratio independently of profits while values greater than 1 would serve to support the hypothesis for the wrong reasons. Even a small number of these perverse observations could serve to overwhelm the industry results where the number of observations are not great. In this sense the retention ratio emerges as a poorly specified variable. A solution to this problem is adopted in the next chapter where I shall use grouped data for the retention ratio in the probit model and omit these two extreme groups. In this way it may be possible to capture the discretionary element to retention policy and the way it might affect the valuation ratio and the probability of takeover.

With liquidity, I expected that highly liquid firms would be taken over although noting the possibility that low liquidity (i.e. high levels of short, term debt) could signal the firm was actually or potentially in trouble and hence a takeover candidate who would not be expected to put up much resistance if an offer was made. While undoubtedly excess liquidity has provided a motive for takeover, it would appear such an effect is being swamped by the role low liquidity plays as a symptom of problems elsewhere in the firm. This is demonstrated by the fact that when the parameter estimate for liquidity is significant it is negative in regressions 1 to 3 and positive in regressions 4 to 6.* From table 4.3 it can be noted, however, liquidity is seldom significant in regressions 1 to 3 although when measured relative to the industry average it improves as an indicator of whether or not the firm is taken over. A somewhat surprising result emerges here. While a liquidity crisis might have been expected to occur immediately prior to the bid and hence liquidity in regression 4 to be more

---

* See the interpretation offered for the sign of liquidity with respect to the furnishing industry in section 4.4, p. 100 above.

important than in regressions 5 or 6 (where liquidity is measured as the average of the two and three years prior to the offer, respectively, divided by the appropriate industry averages), the opposite appears to occur. Liquidity is significant most frequently when it is measured as a three year average in regression 6, declining in frequency by over half to regression 3. Thus it would appear that in a number of industries a liquidity crisis preceded the offer by a few years, the typical acquired firm appearing to have made progress in improving its liquidity up to the time it was taken over. This usually would involve reducing its short term debt, either voluntarily or perhaps more usually at the request of the lending agencies. It is reasonable that this effect should emerge only in the second set of 3 regressions since there undoubtedly exist quite large variations in the average liquidity position of companies stemming not only from changes on the demand side over the trade cycle but also on the supply side resulting from changes in governmental credit control policy over the period. What presumably is happening is that these variations over time are swamping the effect of liquidity in the first 3 regressions while the attempt to remove the variations over time by relating the liquidity position of the acquired firm to the appropriate industry average has allowed the liquidity position to emerge as a significant influence on the probability of takeover. Nevertheless, this effect is still confined to a minority of industries and is not as common as the recent profit record or growth record as an industry influence on takeover.

In table 4.3, the effect of the growth rate virtually disappears when it is measured relative to the industry average. It will be remembered that the growth rate is always measured over the three years prior to the offer if the firm is taken over, so no significance should be attached to the marginal increase in the number of industries for which it is significant between regression 2 and regression 3. Presumably the reason why the relative growth rates in regressions 4 to 6 performed so poorly is that as a long-term measure of past performance, it operated reasonably well as an indicator of whether or not the firm would be taken over but when it was taken relative to the industry average in the second set of regressions, the effect was swamped by the inclusion in the denominator of large variations in industry growth rates over time. This did not seem to happen to the profit rate as the second set of regressions performed only slightly worse than the first. It will be remembered that profits here were measured before tax. I also tried after tax profits and cash flow in place of pre-tax profits which involved running 12 additional regressions for each industry. These results are not included in this chapter since they were basically similar and if anything slightly worse performers than pre-tax profits as an indicator of takeover.

To summarise the results in this chapter, it would appear that while either profits or growth (or both) emerged as significant and with the theoretically anticipated sign in a majority of industries, the firm's retention policy as estimated seemed to have little effect on whether or not it was taken over. Liquidity seemed to play a role in the takeover process such that the less liquid relative to the industrial average were taken over, but it appeared that the liquidity crisis tended to occur some time prior to the offer. An explanation for this was not immediately apparent. By comparison with the results in the previous chapter, it would appear that the valuation ratio provides a slightly more consistent indicator of whether or not a firm will be taken over. Although it was noted in the previous chapter that the coefficient of determination corrected for degrees of freedom ($\bar{R}^2$) will understate the 'true' goodness of fit in the sense described there, this statistic will be comparable for the results of the two models as will the F statistic. By comparison of the two summary tables (3.3 and 4.3) it can be seen that even ignoring the logarithmic formulation of the valuation ratio, there are 39 industries where the valuation ratio proved to be significant but only at best, 22 where profits and 27 where growth emerged as significant. However, the previous discussion of the effects of multicollinearity in the equations of model II should be kept in mind for it was noted there that 40 industries had either profits or growth (or both) as significant; the multicollinearity leading to a high degree of indeterminacy in the estimated equations.

Comparing $\bar{R}^2$ between the two models, I find that in 33 industries, the regressions in table 3.2 with the valuation ratio in a linear form have the best fit, while for the same number of industries, the financial characteristics of the firm provide the best fit of the relationship. With the F statistic, the valuation ratio model performs slightly better with 36 industries having higher F values for the equations in table 3.3 as compared to the equations in table 4.3, while only 30 industries had higher F values for the financial characteristics model. Thus the valuation ratio model appears to perform only slightly better than model II. What does emerge as interesting from a comparison of the two models is that 24 industries have both significant valuation ratio coefficients and either significant profit rate or growth rate (or both) coefficients when regression 1 is compared for both models, and 10 industries have none of these significant.

I have already attempted to discover whether there were any shared characteristics of the industries for which the valuation ratio failed to emerge as significant. I shall now present the results for a similar analysis of the 26 industries for which neither profits nor growth were significant. In doing so I shall also see if there are any characteristics in common of the 24 industries for which both models performed well, as well as the 10 industries for which neither model could produce significant influence on the probability of takeover in terms of the valuation ratio, profits or growth. In table 4.4 appear the number of industries for which neither the profit rate nor the growth rate in model II emerged as significant in ranked groups of industry characteristics. Table 4.5 offers a similar analysis for the 10 industries for which neither the valuation ratio in model I nor either the profit rate or growth rate emerged as significant. Finally, table 4.6 presents a similar breakdown for the 24 industries for which both the valuation ratio in model I and either the profit rate or the growth rate (or both) in model II were significant.* In each case the industry characteristics were ranked from lowest to highest.

The most striking feature to emerge from the industry analysis contained in the three tables below is the failure of any of the industry characteristics to indicate any sort of apparent similarities in (a) the 26 industries for which neither profits nor growth were significant, or (b) the 10 industries for which neither the valuation ratio nor either profits or growth were significant,

---

* This is the same procedure adopted in the previous chapter for the analysis of industry patterns in the non-significant valuation ratio coefficients in table 3.4.

TABLE 4.4

Number of Industries where Neither the Profit Rate nor the Growth Rate were Significant (Regression 1) for Ranked and Grouped Industries by Industry Characteristics

Industry characteristics	Ranked industries						
	1–11	12–22	23–33	34–44	45–55	56–66	Total
Growth rate	5	2	3	6	5	5	26
Size	6	4	3	5	4	4	26
Valuation ratio	3	6	5	2	4	6	26
Profit rate	4	4	4	3	7	4	26
Proportion of T–O's	5	1	5	6	6	3	26

TABLE 4.5

Number of Industries where neither the Valuation Ratio nor either the Profit Rate or Growth Rate were Significant (Regression 1) for Ranked and Grouped Industries by Industry Characteristics

Industry characteristics	Ranked industries						
	1–11	12–22	23–33	34–44	45–55	56–66	Total
Growth rate	2	1	2	0	2	3	10
Size	3	3	0	3	1	0	10
Valuation ratio	2	3	0	1	1	3	10
Profit rate	2	1	2	1	2	2	10
Proportion of T–O's	3	1	1	2	2	1	10

TABLE 4.6

Number of Industries where both the Valuation Ratio and either (or both) the Profit Rate and/or the Growth Rate are Significant (Regression 1) for Ranked and Grouped Industries by Industry Characteristics

Industry characteristics	Ranked industries						
	1–11	12–22	23–33	34–44	45–55	56–66	Total
Growth rate	3	7	4	3	4	3	24
Size	2	5	6	4	5	2	24
Valuation ratio	5	3	5	7	2	2	24
Profit rate	2	6	6	6	3	1	24
Proportion of T–O's	4	5	4	4	4	3	24

or (c) the 24 industries for which both the valuation ratio and either (or both) the profit and/or the growth rate were significant. In the analysis of the corresponding table for the non-significant valuation ratio coefficients (table 3.4) in the previous chapter I discussed a number of expectations concerning the patterns which could have emerged from the analysis of the industry characteristics. Many of the same expectations would have held here because of the theoretically anticipated effect the profit rate and growth rate have on the valuation ratio. There, as here, none of the previous expectations appear to have emerged. The only tentative pattern appearing is in table 4.6 where there is a slight tendency for the industries with the lowest median profit rates and the highest median profit rates to perform less well according to the hypothesis than the middle groups. Unfortunately, an explanation of why both extremes should perform in this way (as with the slight tendency for the extremes in profit rate in table 3.4 to show a greater proportion of industries with non-significant valuation ratio coefficients) is not immediately apparent.*

The results contained in this chapter are, on the whole, similar to those found by the only other major researcher in the field, Ajit Singh. It is not possible to comment upon whether or not the results for the earlier period as contained in his study more strongly suggest influences on the probability of takeover because of the differing statistical techniques employed. Nevertheless, Singh found, using univariate analysis, profits to be the best discriminator of the acquired and non-acquired firms although growth also emerges as a significant discriminator. With retentions and liquidity he is not able to reject his null hypothesis that the two groups of firms are indistinguishable. With multivariate analysis, he was frustrated by the inter-correlations between the variables in improving the discrimination above that achieveable by profits on their own. In this sense, the results achieved here show some improvement on Singh's. This is undoubtedly due to the way in which the industry variations were removed through the specification of

* The reader may wish to remind himself of the previous discussion of table 3.4 in section 3.4 pages 77–80 where, as here, no strong industry pattern emerged. We shall not however, devote any additional discussion to these results because of their apparent random nature.

much finer industry classes. Unfortunately, attempts to discover patterns in the industry analysis were almost completely frustrated. Even with the best of Singh's results, as in the results contained in this chapter, there remains a high degree of indeterminacy in the financial characteristics equations.

Neither the financial variables nor even the valuation ratio provided a complete picture of the characteristics of acquired as opposed to non-acquired firms. Nevertheless, profits, growth and the valuation ratio have here emerged quite consistently as significant influences on whether or not the firm is taken over. Thus not only is it demonstrated that the stock market has an important influence on the probability that a firm will be taken over, but so also does the firm's financial performance and hence to some degree the financial decision policies of the management. It appears as though the firm can go some way towards avoiding being taken over by achieving high growth rates or high profit rates or both. These results by themselves offer little towards an understanding of the appropriate theoretical model of the firm. I previously indicated* that the empirical demonstration of the valuation ratio takeover relationship provided only a necessary condition for the acceptance of the Marris growth maximisation revision to the theory of the firm. Similarly with the results contained here, I cannot say that because it appears a firm can avoid being taken over by seeking high profits or high growth (or both) that they are attempting to do one or the other (or both). It is hoped to shed some light on this question in chapter 6, but first I shall explore the impact of the variables which influence whether or not a firm is taken over individually by means of an alternative statistical estimational technique, that of probit analysis.

* See section 3.5.

5 The Probit Model
of Takeovers:
Aggregate Analysis

5.1 INTRODUCTION

In this chapter I shall attempt to examine some of the variables previously employed in models I and II in a univariate context with all the 3566 firms taken together so that industry classes are ignored. There are several reasons why I choose to examine takeovers in this way which stem from the earlier results. First, I shall look at the impact of each of the variables by themselves because of the multi collinearity problem discussed in the previous chapter with respect to profitability and growth. Furthermore, the causal relation between the financial variables and the valuation ratio indicated treatment in separate models which will be continued here. Second, while the employment of fine industry classifications was indicated by the large inter-industry variations in performance, the results showed neither any general improvement when variables were related to appropriate industry averages nor any indication of patterns in whether an industry would fit or fail to fit the theoretically anticipated relationship. Ignoring the industry classes by taking all firms together into a univariate analysis will undoubtedly have the effect of reintroducing considerable 'noise' into the analysis. This should not lead to biased results because of the apparently random character of the industry results as to whether or not the anticipated relationship would hold in a given industry. The nature of the probit transformation will tend to counteract the effect of the reintroduction of inter-industry variation, as it involves using grouped data.

I shall first in section 5.2 describe the probit technique of estimation and its interpretation with respect to the theory of takeovers put forward by Marris. In section 5.3 I shall present the results and conclusions stemming from this alternative analytical process.

5.2 THE PROBIT TRANSFORMATION AND THE THEORY OF TAKEOVERS

The probit transformation has a long history in biometrics and has recently been applied to economic problems.* For simplicity of exposition, consider the two main variables in the analysis, the dummy variable representing the occurrence or non-occurrence of a takeover and the valuation ratio. At a given level of valuation ratio a certain proportion of companies will be taken over while others will survive. This implies there are variations between firms in their ability to resist a takeover bid. These variations may stem from a number of sources such as the dispersion of share ownership or factors involved in the industrial setting. The essential point is that for every firm there exists a lethal level of valuation ratio, below which it is bound to be taken over and above which it is safe. (The lethal level of valuation ratio is given for firms which are taken over by that level which prompted the offer). For a number of unspecifiable, unknown or random reasons, however, there will exist variations between firms in their lethal level of valuation ratio One may interpret this as a strong form of the Marris valuation ratio constraint. (In the previous analysis of chapters 2 and 4, I was dealing with the hypothesis in a weak form, i.e. the lower the valuation ratio the greater the probability of takeover.)

Assuming the frequencies of lethal levels of valuation ratios are normally distributed, then for a given level of valuation ratio, the normal curve will be divided into two parts. The two areas underneath the curve are determined by the distance of the valuation ratio from the mean when expressed in terms of the standard deviation. The area to the left of this given valuation ratio gives the proportion of firms whose lethal level of valuation ratio is below the given level and the area to the right gives the proportion of firms which will survive with a given ratio.

---

* The major work in this field is Finney (1952). For a step by step account of this method see Mather (1965). Two economic examples using the probit technique may be found in Warner (1962) and Cramer (1962).

Plotting the proportion of firms taken over against the valuation ratio yields a sigmoid. But plotting the normal deviates which correspond to the proportion of firms taken over, a straight line in relation to the valuation ratio is obtained. It often turns out that the frequency distribution of individual reactions is not normally distributed. When, however, the logarithm of the stimulus (in this case, the valuation ratio) is used, the frequencies of the reaction (takeover) becomes approximately normal. A double transformation then yields the desired linear relationship. To remove the negative sign, 5 is normally added to the normal deviates and the resulting values called probits. Thus a probit less than 5 corresponds to a probability of less than 0·5. Regression analysis can then be used on the transformed data. A problem of this technique as it stands is that the variance of the proportion is dependent on the proportion itself. A system of weighting each proportion must be employed before regressing the probit value on the log valuation ratio. The derivation of the proper system of weighting each proportion uses the methods of maximum likelihood.*

An iterative method is used to fit the regression line in the calculation of the best fit. A provisional set of expected values is obtained from a visual fit of a straight line to the transformed data. These expected values are then used with regression analysis to generate expected values for the calculation of a more exact line. If the visual fit was reasonably good, additional approximation of the best fit with further rounds of regression analysis is often unnecessary, two rounds usually proving to be sufficient so that no further improvement in the fit occurs. In fact, the limit to which these estimates tend, as the cycle of determining a new line with the aid of that last calculated is indefinitely repeated, is the maximum likelihood estimate. This procedure is illustrated in the next section prior to the results being presented. Standard errors may be calculated for the parameter estimates and a χ^2 test used as a test of significance.

The probit transformation suffers from none of the defects of the linear probability function employed previously. The problem of heteroscedasticity has been removed by the system of weighting and it is obvious that the calculated value, by

---

* For this derivation see Goldberger (1964) pp. 248–55.

definition, is kept within the interval 0 to 1 so that no anomalies are generated in its interpretation as was possible previously. One is, however, dealing with grouped data and in this sense losing information by the process of grouping. The extent of this 'loss' can be minimised if sufficiently small groups are constructed. I shall explore the sensitivity of the results to changes in group size and number in the next section.

I have limited myself to a univariate analysis (although it is possible to extend the technique to handle any number of independent variables)* because the number of firms necessary to get a satisfactory number of groups, each with a satisfactory number of firms, would exceed the size of the population of public quoted companies. For instance, if one wished to look at two independent variables, e.g. profits and growth, and one wished 15 groups each comprised of at least 50 firms, it would require a minimum of 12,250 companies in the sample (i.e. 15 by 15 by 50) while one is limited to the 3566 firms actually in the population of public quoted companies. In any case, I argue earlier that not only should the valuation ratio be treated on its own,† but also that univariate analysis is appropriate to break the correlation between the other financial variables.‡ The cost of this strategy however may be the introduction of specification bias.

5.3 ANALYSIS, RESULTS AND CONCLUSIONS

I shall first illustrate the probit technique of estimation with an examination of the valuation ratio takeover relationship. The results for all variables employed in the probit analysis will follow and finally I shall offer some concluding remarks on the impact of these results on the analysis in the preceding chapters. This will serve to summarise the results of the examination of the acquired firms, which is concluded in this chapter.

The first step is to categorise all the firms into groups by valuation ratio and to count the number of firms in each group and the number of these which were taken over. A procedure of trial and error is necessary in order to construct the groupings so that there is a reasonable number of firms in each group so that

* For an exposition of this see Finney (1952) p. 105.
† See section 3.2.
‡ See section 4.4.

the proportions are not easily distorted by one or two unusual observations and also that the observations are spread over a reasonably large number of groups. I aimed at achieving around 15 groups each containing approximately 50 firms at the minimum.* The proportions of firms taken over to the group total (Q) and $P = (1 - Q)$ are constructed and the log of the midpoint of each group found. The proportion surviving, (P), is then used to find from tables† the empirical probits (i.e. 5 added to the values of the normal deviates corresponding to the proportions). These empirical probits are then plotted against the log of the valuation ratio group mid-points and a provisional regression line fitted by eye. Expected probits (Y) are now read off from the visually fitted regression line corresponding to the log valuation ratio. These are used to calculate working probits (Y_w) which will be used in regression analysis. The working probit is found from tables which usually need interpolation and are based on the expected probits (Y) and the proportion of takeovers in each group (Q). Weighting coefficients (W) are constructed from tables to weight each working probit which may be regarded as equivalent to saying that each point has been observed W times.‡ Weighted regression is then used as the provisional line in the calculation of a second and presumably better fitting regression line. This second or any subsequent round of calculation is often unnecessary if the visually fitted line was reasonably good. Table 5.1 offers an illustration of the calculations involved in 2 rounds of regressions of the probit transformation on the regression 1 data in chapter 3 for the valuation ratio. The figure above it shows the plotted data with the visually fitted regression line and the first probit regression line.

The first probit regression line is:

$$Y = 2 \cdot 9836 + 2 \cdot 2059X$$
where X is the log valuation ratio

* The data contained in tables 1.8a–1.8c are of the form required for this analysis.
† Tables are available in a number of sources including Fisher and Yates (1943) and Finney (1952).
‡ A complete description of the calculation of working probits and the appropriate weighting coefficients are to be found in Finney (1952) chapters 3 and 4.

using the χ^2 test I find this line accounts for 87·6 per cent of the variation in the probit value.

The second round probit regression line is:

$$Y = 2·93980 + 2·25210X$$
$$(0·04266) \quad (0·01042)$$

This line accounts for 92·5 per cent of the variation in the probit value and with an F value of 162·312 decisively rejects the null hypothesis that no relation exists between the two variables.

From table 5.1 and the figure below it, one can see that the logarithmic transformation of the valuation ratio was appropriate in that the scatter of probit values lie very close to a straight line. The second fitted regression line showed some slight improvement on the first since the visually fitted line overestimated the true slope. It can also be seen that the calculated values from the second probit regression differ only

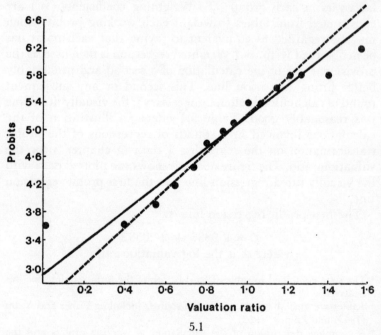

5.1

Note: Broken line is visually fitted regression line and the solid line is the first approximation of the fit by regression.

TABLE 5.1

Probit Regression Calculations for the Valuation Ratio

V-R	log V-R	No. of Co.'s	No. of T-O	P	Q	Y	Y (visual)	Yw	W	Y (calc.)	Yw	W	Y (calc.)
0·10	0	40	37	0·075	0·925	3·5605	2·55	5·9637	2·2536	2·9836	4·0061	5·1080	2·9398
0·25	0·3979	98	89	0·092	0·908	3·6715	3·60	3·6751	29·5950	3·8613	3·6925	38·3592	3·8359
0·35	0·5441	135	116	0·141	0·859	3·9242	4·00	3·9270	59·2151	4·1838	3·9526	67·1693	4·1652
0·45	0·6532	220	172	0·218	0·782	4·2210	4·24	4·2217	112·1032	4·4245	4·2340	123·9788	4·4109
0·55	0·7404	264	187	0·292	0·708	4·4524	4·52	4·4552	156·0636	4·6168	4·4583	159·2395	4·4073
0·65	0·8129	235	135	0·426	0·574	4·8134	4·71	4·8140	146·6706	4·7768	4·8139	146·8233	4·7705
0·75	0·8751	279	139	0·502	0·498	5·0050	4·88	5·0056	176·7409	4·9140	5·0053	177·0618	4·9106
0·85	0·9294	252	116	0·540	0·460	5·1004	5·02	5·1003	160·4156	5·0338	5·1004	160·2317	5·0329
1·00	1·0000	447	160	0·642	0·358	5·3638	5·20	5·3604	280·4567	5·1895	5·3601	280·7786	5·1919
1·20	1·0792	373	133	0·643	0·357	5·3665	5·42	5·3647	220·9354	5·3642	5·3660	226·0716	5·3703
1·40	1·1461	277	76	0·726	0·274	5·6008	5·60	5·6007	154·5328	5·5118	5·5984	160·1780	5·5209
1·60	1·2041	212	46	0·783	0·217	5·7824	5·76	5·7817	108·0267	5·6397	5·7751	116·1209	5·6516
1·85	1·2672	231	50	0·784	0·216	5·7858	5·90	5·7799	108·9026	5·7789	5·7852	117·5143	5·7937
2·50	1·3979	306	66	0·784	0·216	5·7858	6·27	5·6571	110·4721	6·0672	5·7416	127·2532	6·0880
3·50	1·5441	79	7	0·911	0·089	6·3469	6·66	6·2494	17·2117	6·3897	6·3451	24·1329	6·4173

slightly from the first, indicating that the first regression line was a reasonably accurate representation of the probit relationship. Using these calculated values one can generate expected proportions of firms which will be taken over for given levels of valuation ratio. These appear in table 5.2 below along with the actual proportions of firms taken over.

It can be seen that one can use the calculated probit regression line to predict the proportion of firms which will get taken over at any given level of valuation ratio and in this sense consider the additional risk that a firm undertakes if it allows its valuation ratio to fall. I shall discuss this further following the presentation of the full results for the financial variables of profits, growth and retentions and an analysis of the sensitivity of this technique to group sizes.

Table 5.3 gives the results for the probit regressions on the valuation ratio (measured as in regression 1 chapter 3), profits before tax (measured as in regression 1, 2 and 3 in chapter 4), growth (measured as in regression 1 chapter 4), and retentions (measured as in regressions 1, 2, and 3 in chapter 4). The extreme groups of the retention ratio (i.e. negative values and values exceeding 1) were excluded in the three regressions run with retentions because of the problems arising out of the interpretation of these extreme values previously discussed in section 4.4.* This reduces the number of groups for retentions but improves the specification of the variable. Size and liquidity have not been included because an inspection of the probit groups† showed little relationship to exist and also with liquidity, problems would have been created in attempts to impose the logarithmic transformation because of negative values. Regression lines for profits after tax and cash flow were also calculated but proved to perform marginally worse than pre-tax profits, and so are not shown. In all cases, two rounds of regressions were undertaken; the results of the final round are shown in the table.

The most noticeable point from these results is the great improvement over the results from the linear probability func-

* See pp. 103–4.
† Table 1.8a shows the probit groups for size. It was noted in section 1.5, page 27 that no relationship emerged from an inspection of the probit groups for liquidity.

tion employed in chapters 3 and 4. On their own the valuation ratio, pre-tax profits and the growth rate each accounted for over 90 per cent of the variation in the probit value representing the proportion of firms surviving at various values of each variable. As indicated from the standard errors, all variables are significant at the 5 per cent level. Retentions performed less well than the other variables, but remarkably better than in the linear probability model where they were significant in only a handful of industries in regressions 1 to 3. These results are the more surprising since any industry effect on the levels of the variables and the chance of takeover has been ignored in this analysis. These results suggest one can place a high degree of confidence in the predicted values of the proportion of firms likely to get taken over with various valuation ratios, profit rates and growth rates although it must be remembered that the actual proportions are the result of examining takeovers over a thirteen year period. In this sense the intercept is time-dependent as the proportions will increase as the time period is increased.

TABLE 5.2

Expected and Actual Proportions of Takeovers for Given Levels of Valuation Ratio

Expected probit value	Log V–R	V–R	Expected Q(T–O/N)	Actual Q
2·9398	0	0·10	0·980	0·925
3·8359	0·3979	0·25	0·878	0·908
4·1652	0·5441	0·35	0·798	0·859
4·4109	0·6532	0·45	0·722	0·782
4·6073	0·7404	0·55	0·653	0·708
4·7705	0·8129	0·65	0·591	0·574
4·9106	0·8751	0·75	0·536	0·498
5·0329	0·9294	0·85	0·487	0·460
5·1919	1·0000	1·00	0·424	0·358
5·3703	1·0792	1·20	0·356	0·357
5·5209	1·1461	1·40	0·301	0·274
5·6516	1·2041	1·60	0·257	0·217
5·7937	1·2672	1·85	0·214	0·216
6·0880	1·3979	2·50	0·138	0·216
6·4173	1·5441	3·50	0·078	0·089

Note: The values in this table refer to the valuation ratio as measured in regression 1 in chapter 3.

TABLE 5.3

Probit Regression Results

Independent variable	Constant	Parameter estimate	F	R^2	No. of Groups
Valuation ratio (reg. 1)	2·9398 (0·0427)	2·2521 (0·0104)	162·312	0·9250	15
Pre-tax profits (reg. 1)	4·2254 (0·0880)	0·8400 (0·0745)	124·192	0·9324	11
Pre-tax profits (reg. 2)	4·3000 (0·0479)	0·7852 (0·0409)	363·597	0·9762	11
Pre-tax profits (reg. 3)	4·3703 (0·0646)	0·7137 (0·0549)	169·024	0·9494	11
Growth rate (reg. 1)	4·4263 (0·0616)	0·8372 (0·0754)	186·106	0·9539	11
Retention ratio (reg. 1)	4·6865 (0·1160)	0·3643 (0·0749)	23·651	0·7472	10
Retention ratio (reg. 2)	4·7020 (0·1233)	0·3412 (0·0794)	18·454	0·6976	10
Retention ratio (reg. 3)	4·7894 (0·1294)	0·2762 (0·0834)	10·971	0·6105	9

Note: Standard errors appear below the parameter estimates in brackets.

Nevertheless, for taken over firms these results can be interpreted in terms of short-term values of the variables since they were measured at the pre-bid levels. The proportions themselves in table 5.2 no doubt overstate the actual danger of letting the valuation ratio fall, for not only are the proportions time-dependent, but also for surviving firms the valuation ratio is measured as the average over all available years. Thus, returning to table 5.1, the three firms whose average valuation ratio was between 0.0 and 0.2 (i.e. the first group whose mid-point is 0·1) but who were not taken over, maintained that average for a long period of time. Others may have dipped into that class but managed to recover so as to be classed in a higher group and survive. Nevertheless, the clear indication from the results of the probit valuation ratio model is that a falling valuation ratio will increase the chance of a firm being taken over without placing a numerical value to the likelihood. This is firm support for

Marris's theory of takeover and the valuation ratio constraint in its weak form: that the valuation ratio is inversely related to the probability of takeover. Because of the nature of the probit technique, it is also support for a strong form of the constraint. The interpretation of the probit transformation is that there are variations between firms' abilities to resist or avoid a takeover bid which may stem from unspecifiable or unalterable factors.* For all firms, however, there exists a lethal level of valuation ratio although there are variations between firms in this lethal level. Thus, any given firm in given circumstances will be likely to treat this lethal level as a constraint in the sense of the strong form of Marris's hypothesis: that if the firm allows its valuation ratio to fall below a certain level it is almost bound to be taken over, but above this level it is virtually safe from the threat of takeover. As previously noted, however, I can say nothing from the verification of the existence of the constraint (strong or weak) about the nature of the managerial motivations.†

With regard to the financial variables results in table 5.3, both profits and growth are highly significant in explaining whether or not firms get taken over. Like the valuation ratio, both take on the expected positive sign such that the greater the profit rate or growth rate, the greater the proportion of firms which survive. Consequently, as one moves down the groupings for each variable the greater will be the proportion of firms whose lethal level of profits and growth is reached. Furthermore, it appears the two and three year average pre-bid profit rate for firms taken over provides a slightly better explanation of the differences in the proportions that survive at various levels of profit rates than does the profit rate immediately prior to the offer. That is, the probit value associated with the proportion of firms that survive is slightly more closely linearly related to the log of pre-tax profits two and three years prior to the bid if the firm was taken over than it was to the log of pre-tax profits in the year prior to the offer. This is a somewhat different result from that found previously where profits immediately prior to the offer in regression 1 were significant in more industries than either profits in regression 2 or regression 3. It is possible to

---

* This point was made previously with respect to the large residual variance to the linear probability equations; see section 4.4, p. 101.
† See section 3.5.

interpret the extremely good fit of both profits and growth in the manner suggested in the previous chapter with regard to these two variables. That is, to the extent that the profit rate and growth rate are independent such that management has some freedom to maximise one or the other, they can achieve satisfactory levels of security by choosing a satisfactory level of profits (i.e. one which exceeds their lethal level) and seeking a maximum growth rate or vice versa, or high levels of both. Unfortunately, the analysis can shed no further light on the question of managerial motivations and the optimum choice of theoretical model of the firm. I shall return to this question in the next chapter.

With regard to the retention ratio, again the results show a highly significant positive logarithmic relationship with the probit value associated with the proportion of firms which survive. The explanatory power, however, is in no case as impressive as with the previous three variables considered, accounting at best for just under 75 per cent of the variation in the probit value. It appears from the results that the retention ratio in the year prior to the offer for firms taken over (regression 1) is more closely log-linearly related to the probit value than either the two or three year average prior to the offer (regressions 2 and 3, respectively). The positive sign to the relationship between the log retention ratio and the probit value associated with the proportion of firms which survive goes contrary to expectations developed previously in section 2.6. There I anticipated that a high dividend ratio (low retention ratio) would be pro-survival not only because it would, in general, be expected to positively affect the valuation ratio but also it would be a sign of management's expected improvement in future earnings. On the other hand, it was argued a high retention ratio would tend to be required by firms earning low profits to undertake replacement investment and a low dividend ratio would be taken by the market as a sign of pessimistic management. The opposite is suggested by the results, i.e. high retentions are associated with high chances of survival. One explanation for this is that the market favours growth in earnings rather than dividends* and thus prefers the capital gains that

* This suggestion has been made and verified with regard to growth industries by Puckett and Friend (1964).

would result from the high earnings generated from the investment undertaken with retained profits. Thus high retentions
would tend to be associated with growing and/or profitable
companies which previously have been shown as survival prone.
High dividends would therefore tend to be associated with
companies which have few possibilities for growth or profitable
investments and who therefore pay out 'excess' earnings. It
must be stressed that this analysis is only tentative. One would
need additional evidence to support it as an explanation of the
results for the retention ratio contained here.

One possible explanation for the remarkably good fit
achieved by using probit analysis for the financial variables and
the valuation ratio is that the procedure of classing the firms
into a small number of groups has resulted in removing much of
the variation so as to give a misleading impression of the
strength of the true relationship. Although removing random
variation to expose an underlying relationship is usually
desirable especially in cross-section investigations, the strength
of the probit model, in addition to its interpretive relevance to
the takeover hypothesis, is that it overtly recognises and takes
into account the obvious fact that firms (as individuals) vary
in their resistance to a given stimulus (in this case the threat of
takeover). The assumptions that there are variations between
individual firms in the threshold level of stimulus which will
induce the response, that these variations stem from random,
unknown or unquantifiable sources, and that the variations are
normally distributed are precisely the assumptions used to
justify the inclusion of the stochastic error term in regression
analysis. By incorporating these variations in the analytical
technique one can discover directly the otherwise partially
obscured causes of takeover. Nevertheless, I decided to explore
the effect that group sizes and numbers had on the results in
order to discover whether the almost perfect fit uncovered
with respect to the explanatory variables would markedly be
reduced by increasing the number of groups specified in the
analysis. If the residual variation increased dramatically with
increasing the number of groups, one would obviously not be
able to place the same confidence in the results as is possible at
present. Since the valuation ratio is of primary interest to the
analysis of takeovers, I decided to use it as the variable to

examine the effects of increasing the group numbers. The results
previously offered for this variable involved 15 groups. I decided
to subdivide this into 30 and then 60 groups, but when the
results came out I had to settle for 29 and 56 groups, as the
extreme groups had to be combined because there were too
few observations. The results are shown below in table 5.4
along with the previous regression for 15 groups for comparison.
In all cases, two rounds of regressions were undertaken to arrive
at the equations shown in the table.

TABLE 5.4

Probit Regressions on the Valuation Ratio and the Effect of Changing Group Sizes

No. of groups	Constant	Valuation ratio	F	R^2	$\bar{R}^2$
15	2·93980 (0·04266)	2·25210 (0·01042)	162·312	0·9250	0·8633
29	2·93732 (0·15758)	2·26231 (0·15653)	208·875	0·8855	0·8771
56	2·94195 (0·12345)	2·25450 (0·12272)	337·496	0·8621	0·8570

Note: The standard errors of the associated parameter estimates appear
below each in brackets.

It is clear from this table that the earlier results are not
dependent on, or in any way the result of the relatively few
subdivisions of the explanatory variable employed. Both the
slope and the intercept terms remain virtually unchanged. The
F value showing the significance of the equation more than
doubled as the group numbers increase from 15 to 56. The
residual variation increased somewhat as indicated by the R^2
value but when corrected for degrees of freedom, the effect of
increased group sizes actually served to improve the goodness of
fit when the group numbers were increased from 15 to 29. Thus
I conclude from this type of sensitivity analysis of variable
subdivisions that the initial results presented were an accurate
representation of the probit valuation ratio takeover relationship and were in no way dependent upon the group sizes chosen.
In terms of their use as a description of the relationship, the

initial results are perfectly valid, as the subdivisions can be deemed to be sufficiently fine relative to the observable variations in the firm's performance to provide sufficient scope for discussing the result of movements of the variables and the chance of takeover.

The results contained in this chapter reinforce those established in chapters 3 and 4. Of central interest to this investigation is the valuation ratio takeover relationship first put forward by Robin Marris. Both at the industry level where it was found to be significant in a majority of industries and at the agreggate level in the analysis in the present chapter, the inverse relationship between the valuation ratio and the likelihood of takeover (or in the probit model, the positive relationship between the proportion surviving and the log valuation ratio) has emerged. The profit rate and the growth rate similarly emerge as indicators of whether or not the firm will be taken over. Separate analyses were undertaken for the valuation ratio and the financial indicators of performance, for, following Marris, it was expected that the impact of the firm's past performance and present state would be felt via the valuation ratio. It is for this reason he concentrates his attention on the valuation ratio as the primary constraint on managerial behaviour. Having established the existence of this constraint both in its weak form (as a probability function) and in a strong form (as a threshold value which varies normally between firms as in the probit transformation), a necessary condition of the growth maximisation hypothesis with the valuation ratio constraint has been demonstrated. I stressed earlier, however, that these results can do no more in terms of the choice of appropriate theoretical model of the firm. In this sense I have yet to accomplish the third aim of this study, i.e. to relate the takeover phenomenon to the theory of the firm. For this I shall have to examine the raider's rather than the acquired firm's role in the takeover process. This will be done in the next and final chapter.

As noted earlier, had I found perfect separation of the two groups in terms of profits (i.e. no overlap between the taken over and surviving firms), I could have concluded that such a strong control mechanism existed that managers were constrained to seek profits in order to survive. As Singh and others have indicated, positing other objectives to managers if such a strong mechanism was apparent would be trivial for whatever their desires, they would be forced to regard profits as their primary objective. Even in the results in this chapter, no such strong mechanism emerges. Firms can and do survive with low profits and indeed low valuation ratios for reasons outside those the limited* data can uncover. In any case, the functional relationships were established not to attempt to isolate all conceivable causes of takeovers, but to examine those aspects of the firm over whicn management had some degree of control and hence choice: size, profit rate, growth rate, rentention ratio, liquidity ratio, and hence to some extent the valuation ratio. Thus, for example, even though there appeared to be an observable relationship between the age of the firm and its chance of takeover† it was not included as an explanatory variable in the foregoing analytical sections because it can tell us nothing about behaviour. Only if the object was to maximise the discrimination between the two groups would its inclusion be appropriate.

Nevertheless, as indicated in the introduction to this study, the results contained here for the valuation ratio, profits and growth can be used as a basis for discussing the causes of individual takeovers which seems to be the primary objective of many observers of the UK takeover activity. One can undertake descriptions either in terms of their correspondence to the underlying relationships established here or seek explanations of the individual cases if they deviate from the relationships in terms of the extent of the departure and why. Thus the second aim of this thesis, to uncover the underlying causes of takeovers with respect to the firm's performance, has been accomplished.

With regard to the growth rate, both here and in Singh's study it emerged that fast growth can lower the chances of takeover and hence provide a source of managerial security. However, growth has been put forward by Marris as a managerial objective as well. I was not able to get at the precise form of the relationship between objective and constraint because in multivariate analysis I was confounded by the correlation between profits and growth resulting in a high degree of

---

* See section 3.5, pp. 85 where reference is made to Kuehn and Davies (1973) where the concentration of ownership control, a variable only recently available, serves to explain poor performing survival.

† See section 1.5, pp. 31–2.

indeterminacy in the estimated equations. The univariate analysis in the present chapter can give no clues to the inter-actions between the two. An explanation offered is that despite the observed correlation between profits and growth, if manage-ment has a choice between achieving high rates of one and a satisfactory level of the other to achieve a given level of security, then Marris's theory provides grounds for suspecting they will choose to maximise the growth rate. Some minimum or satis-factory level of profits is still necessary to avoid depressing the valuation ratio to an 'unsafe' level or at the extreme to avoid bankruptcy and hence affect the desired level of managerial security.

With regard to the results for the retention ratio, when a comparatively weak relationship finally did emerge in the probit model it took on a sign unanticipated in the earlier theoretical development in chapter 2 and one for which I had no firm explanation to offer. Neither liquidity nor size, the final two variables examined, proved to offer any basis for separating the two groups and in fact were dropped in the analysis in this chapter. Both as discretionary variables and as potential in-fluences on the valuation ratio, retentions and liquidity fail to emerge as significant influences on whether or not a firm will be taken over.

The influence of the industry setting was of interest in this study since it was anticipated that the large variations between industries in terms of the variables employed could serve to obscure the underlying relationships. A comparison of the results of the aggregate analysis in this chapter and the stratified ana-lysis in the two previous chapters, however, does not support the initial concern. Variables significant in the linear proba-bility function models continue to be significant when the industry classes are ignored in the probit models. Furthermore, the industry differences in performance, in general, fail to indicate the reasons why in the previous chapters some industries seemed to fit the anticipated relationships while others did not. Thus, where I expected to be able to attribute the differences in the industry results to industry characteristics, no such relation-ships emerged. Either additional industry characteristics would be required but for the identification of which the data were not available. or the variations could be regarded as random. It is this second possibility which for convenience was adopted when employing the probit model, for it assumes random differences between firms (some of which could be due to unspecified industry characteristics) in their lethal levels of the variables which will prompt a raid upon them.

6 Takeover Raiders and The Growth Maximisation Hypothesis[*]

6.1 INTRODUCTION

It is the purpose of this chapter and the final aim of this study to see if it is possible for an examination of the raider's role within the takeover phenomenon to shed some light on the appropriateness of Marris's growth maximisation hypothesis to the theory of the firm. Previously we found that little could be established with regard to the theory of the firm from an analysis of the acquired firms except to establish empirically the valuation constraint in the form envisaged by Marris. This, however, did not provide grounds for choosing this revision of the theory of the firm in preference to either the neo-classical formulation or other posited objectives imputed to managers.

In what follows I shall empirically examine some of the derivable predictions from the growth maximising model with reference to a subset of the population of firms which have overtly demonstrated a desire to expand externally.† In fairness to Robin Marris, what follows is not strictly an explicit application of the functional form of his model for in his own

---

* The basis of this chapter was presented at the Warwick Symposium In Industrial Economics, the precedings of which appear in Cowling ed. (1972).

† For this we shall use the 117 takeover raiders, analysed in chapter 1, who have undertaken three or more successful raids within the sample period. It will be remembered we found that neither the number nor value of their raids were related to various indicators of their performance. We shall use this in what follows as a justification for treating these firms as a reasonably homogeneous group of companies.

words, 'through most of what follows we shall write as if internal expansion were the only method of growth ... and merger possibilities are subsumed in specifying the functional forms. Alternatively, the reader may regard our theory as representing an account of the limits on growth rates among firms which do not merge.'* The development in this chapter nevertheless remains an application which he implies would not be contrary to his thesis.

I shall take as my starting point the likelihood that those firms which are observed to be actively striving for external growth via takeovers are a subset of firms whose managers include the firms' growth rate as a major component in their objective function. In the UK industrial climate where takeovers are common and such external expansion is a significant proportion of the total growth of firms, takeovers can be seen as a feasible way for many firms to supplement, or even provide an alternative to, internal growth. If by this reasoning, raiders are firms whose managers view growth as a primary objective, then the predictions from a Marris type growth maximisation hypothesis should be verified by empirical tests made with respect to this subset of possible growth maximisers. Moreover, in the context of the preceding discussion, if the growth maximising theory is to have any relevance it ought to be possible to observe some significant departure from the behaviour of the owner controlled profit maximising firm.† The general procedure adopted in this chapter is, in section 6.2, to derive predictions concerning the proportion of raiders expected to achieve values of various stock market and financial variables greater or less than that achieved by firms in a comparable industrial setting‡ for the two alternative behavioural assumptions of profit maximisation and growth maximisation.§ In section 6.3 these predictions are then examined with respect to the actual proportions found empirically.

---

* Marris (1964) p. 124.
† In what follows I shall only consider the effect of attributing these two possible managerial motivations to raiders. However much of what is argued with respect to the maximisation of the growth rate would hold for the sales revenue maximisation model (Baumol (1959)) and with-

[continued on opposite page

It can readily be seen that not only are the two objectives imputed to raiders crucial in determining the predictions, but so also are the objectives attributed to the group of non-raiding comparable firms. That is, the derived performance predictions for raiders as growth maximisers compared with

---

out too much conceptual difficulty would fit into Williamson's (1964) discretionary model where the growth rate plays an important role in determining the amount of slack available within the system. Moreover profit maximisation is not contrasted with growth maximisation simply to put up a straw man to be knocked down. It is rather seen as an alternative and not unreasonable motivational scheme having as its basis strong owner control over managerial behaviour. We are not directly concerned with an examination of the predictions of the classical long-run profit maximisation model since nearly all behaviour is consistent with this. Instead in order to make the notion of profit maximisation operational we will view profit maximisation in a shorter run sense, stemming from owner's uncertainty of the long run and consequently asserting their high rate of discount of the future upon their manager's actions. That this uncertainty of the long run is present, is confirmed by the evidence presented in table 1.1a, which gives the probability of survival within the sample period. As we have shown, any decision which adversely affected short run performance or market standing, though possibly consistent with the long run maximisation of profits, would tend to preclude the achievement of the long run objective by reducing the probability of long-run survival. If one were to cling to the neo-classical model embodying long run profit maximisation as the appropriate managerial objective, then it would surely require managers (owners) to be ignorant of the vast extent of this overt threat to survival. Consequently, in the following analysis we shall regard the behavioural assumption of profit maximisation in a short run context, because it is the short run optimising behaviour which will determine long run survival.

‡ Relating raiders' performance to their respective industry median values is done to normalise the performance indicators and thereby remove differences which are solely attributable to market conditions.

§ An extremely interesting approach to answering a similar question has been adopted by Reid (1968) where he examines for US data various managers' interest variables and shareholders' interest variables of non-acquirers, occasional acquirers, moderate acquirers, and active acquirers. He finds that companies growing by merger tend to be more oriented to managers' interests than shareholders' interests while in non-merging companies the opposite appears to be the case. One can interpret these results that raiders (as fast growing firms) tend to sacrifice owners' (shareholders') interests in favour of their own interests which is in accordance with the predictions from a growth maximisation hypothesis.

the performance of firms in the raider's own industry may change, depending on the sort of assumptions made concerning these comparable firms' motivational objectives. In what

TABLE 6.1

Summary Table of Derived Predictions

Assumption	Growth rate	Profit rate	Valuation ratio	Retention ratio
Raiders: G.M. Others: P.M.	+	−	0	−
Raiders: G.M. Others: G.M.	+	0	+	−
Raiders: G.M. Others: E.L.M.	+	−	0	−
Raiders: G.M. Others: S.F.	+	0	+	−
Raiders: P.M. Others: P.M.	0	+	−	0
Raiders: P.M. Others: E.L.M.	+	+	−	+
Raiders: P.M. Others: S.F.	+	+	0	0
Actual sign of proportion of raiders with greater or less than the median industry value				
All firms	+(111/117)	0(60/117)	+(87/117)	−(70/117)
All raiders and surviving firms	+(97/117)	−(67/117)	0(63/117)	−(78/117)

Note: Proportions greater than 67/117 or less than 48/117 are significant at the 5 per cent level.

follows I shall consider the effect of imputing four possible motivational schemes to the non-raiding firms: viewing them as growth maximisers, profit maximisers, easy life maximisers (resulting in a high preference for security), and finally as sleepy firms differing only in their degree of inefficiency. In fact the body of non-raiding companies may incorporate firms with all the above objectives and probably companies with others as well. The purpose of specifying the objectives is not to test *their* general validity but rather to introduce a greater degree of rigour into the analysis than would be possible in the absence of any discussion of the group of companies to be compared with raiders. If one finds general agreement between the predictions derived employing the four schemes of categorising non-raiding firms when raiders are assumed to be maximising their growth rate as contrasted with the predictions derived under the assumption that raiders are profit maximisers, then greater confidence can be placed upon the analysis than would be possible had not this specification of motives been undertaken. Possibly a drawback of such an approach is that the amount of *a priori* theorising must necessarily increase in proportion to the detail of the analysis. It is nevertheless hoped that a picture of the raider as a growth maximiser which is distinct from the raider as a profit maximiser will emerge from section 6.2 and at least a majority of the analysis on which the predictions are based will be broadly acceptable. For clarity, the predictions are summarised in table 6.1. A positive sign is given where the prediction is that a significant majority of raiders are expected to exceed their respective industry median for a particular variable. A negative sign is given for the opposite prediction and a zero indicates there is not expected to be any significant difference between the two groups.

6.2 DERIVED PREDICTIONS FROM THE GROWTH MAXIMISATION HYPOTHESIS

A Growth Rate

The primary prediction to emerge from the hypothesis is that a significant majority of raiders (firms observed to be actively seeking growth) should in fact demonstrate growth rates higher than non-raiding firms in a comparable industrial setting. Were this not substantiated empirically, doubt would be cast on the applicability of a theory which postulated growth maximisation as a general managerial objective but failed to fit a set of firms extraneously observable as seeking expansion. It is argued below that this is a general prediction from the growth maximisation hypothesis in the sense that it does not depend upon the four possible motives which will be attributed to the non-raiding firms.

As profit maximisers, comparable firms would be expected to achieve rates of growth consistent with the availability of profitable investment opportunities. Identifying this availability with a normal declining marginal efficiency of capital schedule appropriate to the opportunities available within the industrial setting, net investment would cease when the rate of return equalled the cost of borrowing. The raider as a growth maximiser on the other hand would be expected to undertake raids in excess of that warranted by profitability.* Assuming a limited supply of potentially profitable takeover opportunities, this would involve the raider growing faster than firms which were assumed to be maximising profits. By defining raiders as firms which have undertaken three or more raids within the sample period we have allowed the set of comparable firms to undertake expansion by takeover as well as internal investment. Thus considerations of profitability can result in some raiding but in terms of this prediction active raiding is seen as primarily growth motivated.

If comparable firms are themselves growth maximisers, raiders would still be expected to demonstrate faster growth rates, because, as Marris points out, raiding is subject to fewer constraints than is internal expansion. The raider must only consider the marketability (acceptability) of his equity or his ability to service his loan stock, as these form the majority of the payments made for acquired firms. The internal growth maximiser is constrained not only by the above when he seeks funds for expansion but also by the difficulties and costs involved in borrowing elsewhere and the constraints imposed on internal growth by retentions and the supply of technical

* See section 6.2.B where profitability is integrated into the model.

and managerial expertise which the raider is in a sense purchasing along with the assets of the firm. Firms with growth
oriented managers may be seen as the raiders of the future,
trying to establish themselves so as to alleviate these constraints
and eventually become 'high flyers' in the stock market.

A third assumption about the comparable firms is that they
are easy life maximisers and possess managers who have a high
priority for survival and generally undertake satisficing
behaviour. Their aim is seen as the achievement of 'safe'
levels of performance which is an attempt to insulate themselves,
on the one hand, from the likelihood of bankruptcy or dismissal by the shareholders and, on the other hand, from the
possibility of financial disaster or being taken over themselves
as a result of their undertaking excessive risk by attempting to
grow too fast. Here again, the prediction is that raiders
would grow faster than these comparable firms with this
survival motivation, as only a satisfactory level of expansion
would be necessary to keep their market valuation sufficiently
high to discourage raids or a shareholder revolt and maintain
their market share while avoiding high risk investment projects.

Finally, one could envisage the comparable firms as simply
sleepy firms which are a range of companies differing only in
their degree of inefficiency. The majority either go bankrupt
or are taken over. Some survive through favourable market
conditions or fortuitous decisions made in the past, but in
general seldom perform consistently well over a period of time.
Here one would again predict that such firms would demonstrate possibly an erratic but on average low growth rate so
that the raiders would be expected to grow faster than the
industry average were the industry made up of sleepy firms.

The predictions derived by assuming raiders are growth
maximisers consistently view raiders as growing faster than
comparable firms under the various assumptions concerning the
nature of the objectives of these firms. This prediction differs
from that derived by assuming all firms including raiders are
profit maximisers in that in general the profit maximising
raider would not be expected to demonstrate a faster long-run
average growth rate as compared with the firms in their respective industrial settings. Investment projects undertaken solely
on the basis of expected profitability would not be likely to

result in significant differences between firms' growth rates simply due to the chosen mix between internal and external expansion. Of course, some raiders as profit maximisers would grow faster than firms in their industry as a result of extraneous variations between firms in, for example, the quality of management but not as a result of differing motivations which are by assumption identical. As there is no reason to suppose that managerial expertise which would necessarily result in fast growth is concentrated in the hands of raiding firms, we would not expect to observe a pervasive tendency for raiders to grow faster than firms in their own industry, if one assumes raiders as well as comparable firms are profit maximisers.

The implications of assuming raiders are profit maximisers and comparable firms are growth maximisers will not be examined in this section or in those that follow, as such an assumption bears no likely relationship to reality or the theme of this chapter and remains only a conceptual possibility.

If the comparable firms are assumed to be easy life maximisers or sleepy firms, imputing profit maximising behaviour to raiders would be likely to result in predicting that raiders would grow faster than such firms. Neither of these posited situations are pursued here because of the direct and necessary implications such predictions have on the derived predictions for profitability which are considered in the next section.

B Profit Rate

A second and theoretically associated prediction is that a significant majority of raiders as growth maximisers should earn lower than average profit rates than comparable firms. This is a necessary condition for acceptability of a growth maximisation hypothesis in preference to profit maximisation for two reasons. First, in specifying managerial discretion in terms of the growth rate instead of profits, Marris correctly envisaged a trade-off between growth and profitability whereby firms sought expansion in excess of the level warranted by profitability considerations. Profits only enter the managerial objective function by way of a constraint on the primary growth objective to maintain some minimum level. Second, both predictions of a faster average growth rate and a lower average profit rate are a logical necessity in order to distinguish empirically the two theoretical structures. After all, if raiders tended to achieve above average profit rates as well as faster growth rates, it could be argued that raiders were not attempting to maximise their growth rate but rather were successful profit maximisers achieving fast growth as a consequence. This prediction of a lower average profit rate for raiders as growth maximisers is not, however, general, in that it does depend upon the nature of the particular motives specified for the comparable firms.

If the comparable firms are assumed to be seeking maximum profits it is likely that our derived prediction would hold, because, as argued above, raiders were seen as sacrificing profits in favour of fast growth.

Comparable firms as growth maximisers however would also be sacrificing profits in favour of growth. Theoretically we have no grounds on which to distinguish whether the raiding growth maximisers would have sacrificed more or less of their profits to achieve fast growth than the comparable firms as growth maximisers.

As easy life maximisers, the comparable firms would achieve their desired security partly through the maintenance of a satisfactory profit rate. The easy life maximisers would not earn the maximum achievable level of profits since the easy life would involve putting up with some inefficiency and incurring some slack. But since security forms a major part of the easy life he would not be expected to allow his profits to fall to the extent of the growth maximisers where security enters the function not as an *objective* but as a *constraint*. Thus by comparison, raiders as growth maximisers who have sacrificed profits would be likely to demonstrate lower than average profit rates when compared to firms in their industry made up of easy life maximisers.

Were the comparable firms typified by the sleepy inefficient firm described in the section above, we again have little *a priori* basis on which to distinguish the average profit performance of the growth maximising raider, with his minimum profits constraint, and the sleepy firm who typically gets taken over due to a poor profit record. Some insight may be gained, based upon the empirical evidence in this study, but that still will ultimately depend upon one's personal assessment of the commonness of sleepy firms in the industrial population.

The derived profit predictions for raiders as growth maximisers when compared with firms in their respective industries under various assumptions about the nature of the motivations of the comparable firms do not yield as clear a picture as did the growth rate predictions. No definite predictions could be made with regard to the relative performance of growth maximising raiders when comparable firms are assumed to be typified by sleepy firms or growth maximisers. However, the definite prediction emerges that a majority of raiders will demonstrate lower average profit rates when the comparable firms are assumed to be profit maximisers or easy life maximisers. We shall argue below that assuming raiders to be profit maximisers results in the opposite prediction. That is, profit maximising raiders would be expected to be observed earning higher profit rates than the firms in their respective industries and thereby the two theoretical predictions remain mutually exclusive.

To assume all firms including raiders are profit maximisers would, on general equilibrium principles, appear to imply identical or at least not significantly different rates of return earned within an industry regardless of the chosen mix between internal and external expansion. If, however, profit maximising raiders were simply less risk averse than their counterparts who seldom if ever undertook raids, significant differences in rates of return could result. By assumption, raids are only undertaken on the basis of expected profitability. Even if profit maximising raiders were unable to maintain a higher rate of return in the long run, or came to grief in the medium term as the result of too much expansion, so that the profit expectations were not fulfilled in the long run, there would be a tendency for such firms to demonstrate higher short-run rates of return. This is especially likely to emerge when the period over which the performance is examined contains a much higher level of raiding activity towards the end, so that one would be observing the majority of profit maximising raiders during their short-run period of super normal profits. Furthermore, if one believes that the population of companies comprises a range of firms with profit making potential based either upon the degree of risk aversion or upon differences in managerial talent it would not be unreasonable to accept the widely held view that raiders are dynamic firms with good quality management. Here again, the expectation is that raiders' superior managerial talent, assuming it is directed at maximising profits, would tend to result in a significant majority actually exceeding the median rate of return for their respective industries. If one assumes the comparable firms are easy life maximisers or sleepy firms instead of profit maximisers, this conclusion is all the stronger as these alternative modes of behaviour result in non-optimal profit performance.

C Valuation Ratio

An integral part of the Marris growth maximising hypothesis concerns the trade-off between the growth rate and the firm's valuation ratio. Just as it was argued earlier the growth maximiser would tend to sacrifice profits for growth, he also would be trading off the valuation ratio against his growth rate. He is restrained, however, in his attempts to maximise growth by a security constraint imposed through the valuation ratio. This security constraint is seen as operating because of the previously established inverse relationship between the valuation ratio and the probability of takeover. To the extent that a firm's profit performance affects its market valuation, the trade-off between growth and profits and growth and valuation ratio will amount to the same thing and therefore will involve managers adopting policies designed to maintain some minimum value of both variables for reasons of security. This would imply that internal growth maximisers would tend to have lower valuation ratios than the median of firms in their respective industries. I shall argue below however that because growth maximising raiders achieve their growth objectives externally, a significant number would, for various reasons, tend to display valuation ratios above their respective industry medians.

Not only would growth maximising raiders wish to keep their valuation ratio safe, but they also would wish to keep it high, thereby effectively lowering the cost of the acquisition to the extent that it is financed by a share issue. The desire however, is not sufficient to explain why the market would be expected to favour the growth maximising raiders' shares. Part of the explanation lies in the role retentions play in the determination of market valuation. This will be discussed in detail in section 6.2.*D*. Briefly, I shall argue that raiders would be expected to retain a smaller proportion of after tax earnings (i.e. pay out higher dividends) in an attempt to raise the valuation ratio – high dividends would tend to be valued by the owners and hence the market.* Additionally, to the extent the market is, as Keynes described, a beauty contest, raiding would tend to make the firm known and superficially attractive; thus desired by investors as part of their portfolio. Further, any conglomerate element in the expansion will be recognised as risk spreading and thus desired by investors, in so far as the raider will be less affected by unexpected contractions in demand in one sector. On the other hand, raiders' shares would be in demand by risk takers in so far as some raiders do very well in terms of profits. Finally, to the extent that raiding is financed by loan stock or even convertible loan stock (which we previously noted had come into prominence as a method of payment in the recent takeover boom), and the rate of return earned by the raider exceeds the cost of servicing the loan stock, the share of profits from the acquisitions will tend over time to be diverted to the pre-acquisition owners; though with convertibles this time span will be limited. Thus, despite the fact that the growth maximising raider is sacrificing profits which would normally depress the valuation ratio, the method of expansion by takeover would generally result in the enhancement of raiders' valuation ratios. The security constraint may only be operable when raiders as growth maximisers fail to maintain their growth rate or fail to satisfy their minimum profits constraint, the latter likely causing the former. This explanation is consistent with the observations Marris made that firms are reported to be taken over for attempting to grow too fast and losing control; the poor profit position having caused the firm to retrench and therefore lower its growth target.

In terms of the method of analysis of this chapter, assuming raiders are growth maximisers and the set of comparable firms

---

* See section 2.6 where the role of retentions of the acquired firm was discussed in relation to its affect on the valuation ratio.

are typified by either profit maximisers or easy life maximisers does not allow us to derive definite predictions. Comparable firms as profit maximisers would be able to maintain healthy valuation ratios because of the effect profits have on the valuation ratio. Similarly the easy life maximisers in their desire for security would be forced to keep up the valuation ratio by adopting policies which avoided the threat of takeover or shareholder intervention. Despite the basis for believing that these two motivational schemes would result in high valuation ratios, we have no basis on which to derive predictions in terms of relative levels of the valuation ratio.

If comparable firms are assumed to be growth maximisers, it is likely a significant majority of raiders as growth maximisers would have greater than average valuation ratios. This follows from what was argued in sections 6.2.*A* and 6.2.*B*. Raiders could grow faster than their internal growth maximising counterparts because they faced fewer external and internal constraints. They need not, however, have had to sacrifice their profit rate any more than the internal growth maximiser to achieve the faster growth. Thus raiders' valuation ratios *ceteris paribus* would tend to be higher than the set of growth maximising comparable firms.

If the comparable firms are typified by sleepy inefficient firms, it is also likely that a significant majority of growth maximising raiders would have higher valuation ratios. There is nothing in the sleepy firm's performance to cause the market to favour its valuation of such a firm. Also, this sort of firm is typically taken over because of its low valuation ratio and the fact that alternative management could earn a greater rate of return with the given assets. The sleepy firms that survive raiding most likely are insulated by voting control being in the hands of owner managers or families sympathetic to existing management.* Thus one would expect the raider with its healthy growth rate to command a better market valuation than the sleepy inefficient firm.

If it is now assumed that raiders are profit maximisers the prediction for the majority of raiders' valuation ratios depends upon the accuracy of the argument put forward in section

* See Kuehn and Davies (1973).

6.2.B concerning the profit maximising raiders' short-run and long-run profit performance *and* the time horizon of the stock market. If, because of a lower risk aversion than their profit maximising non-raiding counterparts, profit maximising raiders manage to earn short-run super-normal profits but tend in the longer run to be forced to retrench; and if the market's time horizon is long enough to incorporate the effect of this likelihood into its evaluation of the firm's shares, then the market will tend to discount the present short-run profits in its evaluation of the profit maximising raiders' shares. Thus one could expect a significant majority of raiders as profit maximisers to have valuation ratios below that of profit maximising comparable firms. This is another way of suggesting that the stock market rewards long-run success and stability and tends to be rather cool towards short-run risky behaviour.*

If the comparable firms are easy life maximisers and raiders are profit maximisers, it is likely a significant proportion of raiders would demonstrate lower average valuation ratios than the set of comparable firms. Easy life maximising managers would be expected to maintain healthy market valuations by adjusting their financial indicators so as to gain market (and shareholder) approval. Safe valuation ratios for such managers would then be that level which minimised the threat of takeover and satisfied shareholders so that their job security was guaranteed in so far as was possible. This safe level would be expected to be greater in a significant number of cases than that demonstrated by the raider were he to be maximising profits in that, as argued in the previous paragraph, raiders with a short-run profit objective would not be likely to be able to maintain this in the longer run. This we argued would be reflected in the market's valuation of its shares since the market was seen as being interested in a long run view of performance. Even if the profit maximising raiders do not suffer a fall in profits as a result of raiding but simply display a greater variance, as would be expected from undertaking a risky method of achieving profits, the market again might well be expected to down-

---

* This argument would not apply to growth maximising raiders because their profit rates have not been enhanced in the short run but rather sacrificed. It is their fast growth which is affecting their valuation ratio and is thus a longer term measure of performance than annual profits.

grade the value of such firms' shares. Finally, the market does not necessarily reward firms only on the basis of profitability. Thus, firms earning above average profit rates will not necessarily have above average valuation ratios.* For these reasons, a significant majority of raiders would be expected to have lower average valuation ratios than comparable firms typified by easy life maximisers, whose main vehicle to the easy life is a 'safe' valuation ratio.

If comparable firms are sleepy firms, no definite prediction can be made with regard to their market valuation relative to that of profit maximising raiders. Both categories would tend to possess low average valuation ratios, and there is little basis on which to assert that one group's would be lower than the other.

To summarise, the pattern of the derived predictions concerning the valuation ratio for raiders versus comparable firms, while somewhat tentative and dependent upon the various assumptions made concerning the objectives of comparable firms, yields a reasonably clear cut division between the two posited managerial objectives of growth maximisation and profit maximisation. In the former case, we expected either no significant difference between raiders' valuation ratios and the median value for their respective industries, or that raiders would be likely to possess higher valuation ratios when compared with their industry median values. In the latter case, assuming raiders to be primarily motivated by profitability resulted (in general) in predicting a significant majority of raiders to have their shares valued lower in the market than the median value for their respective industries.

D Retention Ratio

The ratio of retained to total after tax earnings in addition to being a variable determined as the discretion of managers, will also affect the level of the firm's valuation ratio. As with the valuation ratio predictions, the predictions for the retention

---

* Regressions run on each of the 66 industries with average profit rates of the firms as the independent variable and their valuation ratio as the dependent variable showed profits to be significant and take on a positive sign in only 26 industries. Moreover, the explanatory power of the industry equations was in most cases quite low.

ratio differs from that postulated by Marris where growth was limited to that financed internally out of retentions and debt. Internal financing of investment implied that to maximise growth, earnings would need to be ploughed back so that the dividend payout ratio was low – consequently the retention ratio high. Incorporating external growth via takeovers in the growth maximising hypothesis gives us the opposite prediction for the retention ratio. Retentions no longer act as a constraint on growth since most takeovers are financed wholly or in the greatest part by the issue of new shares in exchange for the raided company.*

The choice of retention ratio would then depend upon the dispersion of ownership and control within the firm, or in other words, the degree to which owners are able to impose their own aims on managers. With growth maximising raiders, this dispersion is likely to be great, as indicated by their ability to seek an objective which is not likely to be directly in the shareholders' interests. The choice of retention ratio for growth maximising raiders is more likely to be determined by its role as an influence on the valuation ratio. From the arguments in section 6.2.C in terms of the valuation ratio's role as a security constraint, managers would be expected to feel that low retentions (high dividends) would serve to increase their valuation ratio thereby reducing the threat of loss of job through takeover. Additionally, high dividends in themselves could add to security by removing the likelihood of owners using their alternate sanction on managerial policies; that of dismissal. This prediction that a significant majority of growth maximising raiders will have low average retention ratios when compared to firms in their respective industrial settings is general in the sense that I shall argue that its application to the growth maximising raiders does not depend upon the four alternative motivational schemes applied to the rest of the comparable firms.

If the comparable firms are assumed to be profit maximisers, their retention ratio would depend upon the availability of profitable investment opportunities and the ease and cost of

---

* Where takeovers are financed by the issue of loan stock no great additional demand will be made on retentions providing the raider does not allow itself to become too highly geared, i.e. the ratio of new shares to new loan stock does not change significantly.

acquiring funds elsewhere. Even though owners (who are by assumption able to assert their influence over managers to maximise profits) are likely to have a positive preference for current dividends, it is more likely that they would prefer the gains and higher future dividends that could result from funds being ploughed back into profitable investment projects. Thus profit maximisation is likely to result in high retentions. Therefore by comparison with the growth maximising raider with low retentions, the prediction emerges that a significant majority of raiders will have lower average retentions when comparable firms are assumed to be maximising profits.

Similarly, if comparable firms are assumed to be growth maximisers, raiders would, in general, be likely to retain less, because firms maximising their growth rate but for the most part confining their expansion to that financed internally, would require high retentions and hence pay out low dividends.* Raiders by comparison seeking to enhance their valuation ratio by high dividends would tend to retain less.

If comparable firms are easy life maximisers they would choose their dividend ratio and hence retention ratio to ensure satisfactory security. All discretionary variables which affect (or are believed to affect) the valuation ratio were seen as being chosen with this aim in mind. However, managers would not have to raise dividends to offset the effect on the valuation ratio of the deliberate sacrifice of some other financial variable. They would be likely to choose some level of retentions which gave them sufficient finance for growth but which did not adversely affect the valuation ratio. Growth maximising raiders, however, were seen earlier as having to offset their sacrificed profits by high dividends in order to raise their valuation ratios. Thus the prediction emerges that a significant majority of raiders as growth maximisers would be likely to have low average retention ratios when compared with firms in their respective industries which are assumed to be easy life maximisers.

Finally, if the set of comparable firms is typified by sleepy inefficient firms, growth maximising raiders would again tend

---

* This corresponds to the argument Marris put forward with regard to retentions in support of his growth maximising hypothesis.

to retain less. Since the sleepy firm's profit performance was poor, it would require a large proportion of its meagre earnings simply to invest in replacement capital in order to stay in operation. To the extent that they engage in any positive net investment the demands placed upon retentions from earnings are all the greater. Alternative sources of borrowing to finance replacement investment would usually be either fully exploited or unresponsive since such companies had demonstrated by past performance they were poor risks. Further, it is unlikely that the managers of sleepy firms would have the awareness to attempt to increase their market valuation by raising dividends even if it were possible given their poor record of return on capital employed, as such firms typically are among those taken over because of low market valuation. Growth maximising raiders, it has been argued, would typically have a low retention ratio so that by comparison a significant majority would probably have lower average retention ratios when compared with a set of comparable firms assumed to be sleepy firms.

By examining the alternative motivational scheme of raiders as profit maximisers, a contrasting view of the relative size of the retention ratio as compared with firms in raiders' respective industries results. If all firms are profit maximisers and even if raiders do manage to earn short-run super-normal profits, there is little basis on which to argue that there would be a pervasive tendency for raiders to retain a greater or lesser proportion of earnings than firms in their respective industries. As argued earlier, the retention ratio does to some extent reflect the degree of owner control within the firm. As by assumption all managers are seeking to maximise profits for the owners and thus are assumed to be quite directly owner controlled so that retentions are generally kept high, there is no reason to believe that differences in the average retention ratios for the two groups should emerge simply as a result of differences in the mode of investment activity (i.e. whether internal or external via raids).

Imputing easy life maximisation to comparable firms and profit maximisation to raiders gives the opposite sign prediction than when growth maximisation was attributed to raiders. Easy life maximisers were seen earlier as paying out dividends at a level which would ensure the valuation ratio was sufficiently high to minimise the likelihood of takeover. Profit maximising raiders, however, were seen as paying out a low ratio of dividends to total earnings because of owners' preferences for capital gains and future dividends over present dividends. Thus one would expect a significant majority of profit maximising raiders to display higher retention ratios (lower dividend payout ratios) than firms in their respective industries assumed to be easy life maximisers.

Finally, assuming comparable firms are sleepy firms and raiders are profit maximisers does not allow us to differentiate between the two groups. We have argued that both classes would tend to have high retention ratios but there is no basis on which a comparison can be made in terms of which group would be likely to have a significant majority of greater or lesser retention ratios.

The picture that emerges in terms of the retention ratio is that by imputing growth maximisation to raiders we would expect to observe a significant majority of them with average retention ratios below their industry median. This prediction was not dependent upon the various imputed motives of the managers of the set of comparable firms. Alternatively, by assuming raiders are profit maximisers, we predicted either no difference, or that a significant majority of raiders would be expected to show greater average retention ratios than firms in their comparable industrial settings. Thus, two distinct predictions for the retention ratio have emerged from the starting point of alternative behavioural assumptions imputed to the managers of raiding firms. A further basis then is offered on which the appropriateness of these alternative theoretical models may be judged.

In the arguments in this section, the attempt has been to derive logical implications or predictions from a starting point of assuming firms which can be extraneously identified as seeking expansion externally by takeovers are firms whose managers possess some positive desire for growth in excess of or in place of that which would result from assuming profit maximisation to be their primary behavioural objective. The next section contains a description of the statistical procedure adopted to test the two sets of predictions against reality.

6.3   EMPIRICAL TEST OF THE DERIVED PREDICTIONS

Initially what was desired was to compare each of the four indices of performance of the 117 raiders individually with a group of comparable firms so that variations attributable to the industrial setting would be removed. This was accomplished by relating each of the values of the raiders' variables to their own respective industrial medians. This process was repeated omitting the non-raiding firms which were taken over. Thus, for example, in the case of a raider having a major interest in three industries, the overall median for each variable for this combined 'industry' was compared with the calculated value of each of the raider's performance indices. Finally, the sign test* is employed in order to examine any pervasive tendencies for raiders to demonstrate either high or lower values of the performance variables than their respective industries and to relate these tendencies to the alternative sets of behavioural predictions derived in section 6.2. The sign test is used in preference to parametric tests because it is untenable to assume that the differences between raiders' performance and the performance of companies belonging to the same industrial setting will have the same variances. The null hypothesis we wish to test is that each difference has a probability distribution (which need not be the same for all differences as required by the t-test) with median equal to zero. We will reject the null hypothesis if the number of positive and negative sign differences differ significantly from equality.† Of particular interest is whether the significant proportions of sign differences are in accordance with the theoretical predictions developed in terms of the growth maximisation hypothesis or alternatively, whether the proportions tend to favour the predictions derived on the basis of assuming raiders to be profit maximisers.

---

* For a description of the use of the sign test see Dixon and Massey (1957) p. 280.
† The further assumption is required that the differences between raiders' performance and their industry medians are independent. Even though the existence of a raider in one industry might possible affect the performance of firms in that industry, it is exceedingly unlikely that such a raider would affect the performance of firms in other industries. As the 117 raiders cover 65 of the 67 industries and because of the procedure of multiple industry classes for each firm, only resulting in four industries where there are more than one raider, the independence condition is likely to be satisfied.

6.4   RESULTS AND CONCLUSIONS

Table 6.1 gives in brackets the actual proportions for the most frequently occurring sign of the difference between raider's performance and their respective industry median value for each of the four variables.* Taking the level of significance at which we reject the null hypothesis that no difference exists between the two groups at the 5 per cent level of probability, signs are included corresponding to the most often occurring difference. Zeros indicate that the derived proportions of positive signs to total are not statistically significant.

The overall impression to be derived from these results is that they are more consistent with the predictions derived from the assumption that raiders are growth maximisers than with those derived from imputed profit maximisation. That is, raiders tend to be faster growing than firms in their respective industries but yet this growth has not generated significantly higher profits and indeed when compared with only the surviving firms in their industry, raiders actually earned a lower rate of return on assets. Raiders nevertheless were able to maintain their valuation ratios at healthy levels despite their profit performance. Thus 87 of the 117 raiders had ratios above their respective industry medians when compared to all firms. This fell to 63 when only surviving firms were used in the comparison. The results for retentions possibly indicate how they were able to outweigh the negative influence of their poor profitability on the valuation ratio. Both for comparisons with all firms and surviving firms, raiders had lower retention ratios and thus higher dividend payout ratios than the median of the firms in their respective industries. Logically, one would further expect that if low retentions are playing the role of offsetting the dampening effect sacrificed profits have on the valuation ratio, the raiders with below average profits would tend to be the firms which had the significantly lower retention ratios. By splitting the raiders into two groups comprised of those which exceeded their industry median in profit rates and

---

* Profit rates used were before tax while the valuation ratio was measured using the annual mean share prices in the numerator. When after tax profit rates and annual low share price were used in the numerator of the valuation ratio there was no significant change in the proportions for each variable given in the results.

those which fell short of the industry median, it is found that just under 80 per cent of these latter companies payed out more, (i.e. 43 of the 67 raiders with below their industry median in profit rates when all firms are used in the comparison and 53 of the 67 when only surviving firms are used). Regarding the raiders which earned above their industry median profits, there was no significant difference in retention ratios. The most plausible explanation is that this is consistent with attempts to raise the valuation ratio by paying out high dividends for raiders whose low profits were negatively affecting their market valuation, but this diversion of funds for expansion being unnecessary for raiders with healthy profits. Thus not only were they playing on shareholders preferences for dividends (as well as capital gains) in high payouts when necessary to keep their share prices healthy, but also their past growth record made them appear to be an attractive company to the market. In general they were allowed to pursue their policies towards growth without interference from shareholders or incurring any severe threat of being taken over themselves* due to their healthy market valuation. And as a consequence, in seeking growth they were permitted to trade-off profits without obviously incurring any additional threats to security. By inspection of table 6.1 it can be seen that the alternative view of raiders as profit maximisers (or firms which are significantly owner controlled and thus induced to regard profits to owners as important) does not correspond as closely to the picture of the raider which has emerged from the results. On certain assumptions, the profit maximising raiders may be faster growing, but it is difficult to see how they could emerge as less profitable. Even though when considering all firms in the industry comparisons there is no significant difference in profitability at the 5 per cent level, it must be remembered that within this group are a large number of firms taken over due to poor profit records. Furthermore, since raiding is risky and does not necessarily result in super-normal profits it is difficult to see how the profit maximising raider would tend to keep the high valuation ratios observed, especially since

---

* Only 16 of the 117 raiders, or 14 per cent, were themselves taken over as compared with the average of over 43 per cent of all firms taken over. (See table 1.4).

he is not distributing significantly higher dividends and may on certain assumptions about the comparable firms even be distributing less (i.e. retaining more).

It is left to the reader to draw conclusions concerning which assumptions about the nature of the comparable firms are most appropriate based upon his own judgement of the commonness of each type of firm in the population. Nevertheless, one further stage in the analysis can be made, based upon the assumption that the easy life maximiser has a strong desire for survival. Taking it that this group of comparable firms will arrange their affairs in order to achieve this stated goal it is likely that a majority of such firms will actually be successful and survive. By examining the alternative predictions for growth maximising raiders and profit maximising raiders when comparable firms are easy life maximisers, and comparing each with the results for raiders and the group of surviving firms, a clear contrast of the two motivational schemes becomes apparent. In this case, it can be seen that the assumption of growth maximisation for raiders clearly is more in line with the results than are the predictions based upon the assumption of profit maximisation. That is, when comparable firms were assumed to be easy life maximisers, the assumption of growth maximisation imputed to raiders yielded the predictions that raiders would grow faster, have lower profit rates and retain less – the prediction for the valuation ratio comparisons was uncertain and could have gone either way depending on the strength of counter arguments. On the other hand, assuming raiders to be profit maximisers while the comparable firms were assumed to be easy life maximisers resulted in predicting raiders would grow faster, have higher profit rates, have a lower valuation ratio and retain more. Examining the results for the comparisons of raiders with surviving firms shows the predictions based on the assumption of growth maximisation to be more closely in line with reality than the predictions based on assuming raiders to be profit maximisers.

In this chapter, the attempt has been made to formalise the growth maximisation hypothesis with respect to a subset of the population of firms. Some of the theorising in section 6.2 represents a departure from Marris, though much of what is argued is in accordance with his hypothesis, at least in spirit.

This fragmented approach to the examination of the relevance of this theoretical revision to the theory of the firm was necessary in order to avoid the circularity of assuming the fastest growing firms are growth maximisers, the most profitable, profit maximisers and so forth. At the extreme, had not the derived predictions been supported, then serious doubt would have been cast on the applicability of the growth maximisation hypothesis as a basis for revision of the theory of the firm.

In the present economic climate, takeovers are extremely common, often recently occurring at a rate of around 25 per month of public quoted companies. Raiding is by no means limited to the 117 firms examined in sections 6.3 and 6.4, as not less than 20 per cent of the population of 3566 companies have undertaken at least one takeover at some time during the sample period and that percentage is increasing as raiding activity spreads to other industries relatively untouched previously. The motivations and predictions analysed in section 6.2 could be extended to incorporate these minor raiders as well. Furthermore, it may be the case that raiding itself is limited to relatively large firms, and small concerns must overcome some threshold size in order to indulge in takeover activity. They would, in this case, be forced to adopt policies of internal growth maximisation possibly in preparation for the time when they can also join the takeover scene – in addition to the numerous reasons offered by Marris why they might do so anyway. That to become a 'high flying' raider is desired by firms, I think, is demonstrated by the results; raiding leads to growth, security through safe levels of the valuation ratio, and size, all of which are valued for themselves by managers and also for the rewards, both pecuniary and non-pecuniary associated with growth and size.

Thus, it would be wrong to say the results contained in this chapter are valid only for a limited number of 'special' firms; the implications of the analysis and results are likely to be far more general and consequently add to the growing body of evidence supporting the appropriateness of the managerial and behavioural revisions of the theory of the firm.

Appendix I:

Census Population and
Data Collection Procedures
and Description

I CENSUS POPULATION

The initial population of firms comprises all UK quoted companies exclusive of the following industry groups: foreign mining, rubber and tea plantations, water works companies and electrical and gas suppliers, investment trusts, banks and discount houses, and insurance companies. Firms which were incorporated outside the UK have been excluded although Irish companies which were re-incorporated in Northern Ireland in 1920 have been retained. In addition, companies which were subsidiaries of other companies before 1 January 1957 (the beginning of the time period examined) have been excluded, as have companies which went public or had their shares first quoted after 30 June 1966. Included in this initial population of 4057 companies is what roughly can be termed 'domestic commercial and industrial companies' whose control was at some time in private hands and whose equity is quoted on the London Stock Exchange or any of the UK Associated Stock Exchanges.

From this initial population, several categories of companies have been omitted before arriving at the final population of 3566 companies. These categories are set out in table I along with the number of companies and the number of takeovers in each. Table II provides the annual distribution of takeovers for the main omitted categories and the total annual distribution of takeovers of all omitted firms.

For this study it was necessary to have a population of companies which had their voting equity quoted on any of the

UK exchanges and which if they disappeared, did so because of takeover and for no other reason. This is the general explanation for the omission of categories (1) through (9), though some elaboration is given below.

Category (1) includes 24 companies which came into the population part-way through the period but were previously private and wholly owned subsidiaries of other quoted companies. In these cases, the parent company sought a stock

TABLE I

Analysis of Omitted Companies

Category	No. of firms	No. of takeovers
1. Companies which went public after 1957 as subsidiaries of another company	24	0
2. Companies which were nationalized sources: Transport Holding Co. – 9 British Steel Corp. – 9 National Coal Board – 1 British Sugar Corp. – 1	20	0
3. Companies converted private	2	0
4. Companies for which no accounts were made before they were taken over	2	2
5. Control transfered outside UK	1	0
6. Quotation only on Provincial Brokers Stock Exchange	17	2
7. Voluntary Liquidations and Compulsorily wound-up Distribution by year 1957 – 4 1964 – 21 1958 – 8 1965 – 15 1959 – 10 1966 – 18 1960 – 19 1967 – 20 1961 – 8 1968 – 9 1962 – 11 1969 – 11 1963 – 14	163	0
8. Non-quoted companies and companies whose quotation is granted in non-voting equity only	247	116
9. Companies for which there were insufficient markings of their voting shares on the stock exchange	185	98

exchange quotation for their subsidiaries in order to expand the company's finance but did not release voting control into public hands. For this reason, it was impossible to take over these subsidiaries without the parent company's deciding to sell and consequently they have not been retained.

TABLE II

Distribution of Omitted Takeovers by Year and Category

Year	Non-quoted Companies	Insufficient markings	Total*
1957	8	10	18
1958	13	9	22
1959	13	13	26
1960	13	9	23
1961	9	7	16
1962	19	7	27
1963	14	11	25
1964	2	5	7
1965	8	8	16
1966	7	9	17
1967	6	6	13
1968	4	2	6
1969	0	2	2
TOTALS	116	98	218

* These totals include other categories.

Nationalised companies in category (2) have been omitted as have the two companies in category (3) which were converted to private companies, because the reasons for these disappearances from the list of quoted companies are extraneous to the process of takeover and, as such, are irrelevant to the present thesis. The two companies in (4) were omitted because no accounts were published before they were taken over. In both cases, these were new companies, formed as the result of a merger. The single company in (5) had its control transferred to Jamaica and was reincorporated in that country. It is therefore treated as a foreign company and not retained. The 17 companies in category (6) had their quotation only on the Provincial Brokers Stock Exchange. The markings of companies quoted on this exchange are infrequent and not recorded in the Official List. All the companies are very small and often do not close their books at the end of an accounting year. As stock market and accounting data are required in this investigation, these companies were omitted. Category (7) contains 163 companies which have gone into voluntary liquidation, have been compulsorily wound-up or have had their quotation cancelled by the Stock Exchange and hence have disappeared for reasons other than takeover.

As the process of takeover concerns a change of control via the stock market, companies which possess no quotation for their voting shares are not retained in the final population. The 247 companies in category (8) are therefore omitted. In category (9) are 185 companies which have been omitted because there were too infrequent markings recorded for their voting shares. For some of these companies no markings have been recorded for the last thirteen years while for others there only exists a few annual markings and no share price range within the year. The existence of one price for both the annual high and low usually indicates that the shares had only been traded once in that year. Typically such firms are family businesses in which the directors control a majority of the voting equity.

II DATA COLLECTION PROCEDURES AND DESCRIPTION

Having arrived at the final population, the data was then compiled on 8 × 5 in. cards, one card corresponding to each company. The primary sources are The Exchange Telegraph (EXTEL) Daily Statistical Service and Auxiliary Service, *The Stock Exchange Official Year Book*, and *Who Owns Whom*. In some cases these sources have been supplemented by the published company accounts and share prices from the Financial Times, both of which were made available by EXTEL at their London office.

A Identification of Takeovers

Once the initial population of 4057 companies had been noted, the most recent volumes of the *Stock Exchange Yearbook* and *Who Owns Whom* were consulted to discover which firms had disappeared and whether the disappearance was due to takeover. As set out in section I above, a number of companies disappeared due to reasons other than takeover and were not retained. The balance were takeovers and mergers.

B   Treatment of Mergers

The distinction between takeovers and mergers is that with a takeover, an existing company or individual(s) acquires the capital of another company, while with a merger, a new company is formed to acquire the capital of two or three existing companies. The identification of raider and acquired firm which is obvious when takeover occurs is not obvious in the case of mergers. Some special treatment is necessary if the 39 mergers which have occurred are to be categorised as takeovers. Three methods of distinguishing between the raider and the acquired firm were employed, the results of which are set out in table III below. In each case the first firm listed was deemed to be the raider.

By the first method, the composition of the board of directors of the new company was compared with that of the two or three merged companies in order to ascertain which had the strongest bargaining power when the new company was formed and which therefore gained control of the new company. A system of weighting was employed in which a merged company would receive 3 points if a member of its board became chairman of the new company, 2 points if a member was appointed to any of the following posts: deputy chairman, managing director, joint managing director, or general manager, and one point for each member appointed to a non-titled position on the board of the new company. In 31 cases this method of classification proved conclusive leaving a balance of 8 mergers for which the point totals were the same or differed by one point. Two other methods of classification were to compare the relative sizes of the merged companies in terms or market value and book value. The first of these measures shows which of the merged companies would have voting control of the new company after the shares of the merged companies were exchanged for shares in the new company. (In every case, the merger was accomplished by means of a share exchange.) There was substantial agreement registered between all three methods, and using the second and third methods

TABLE III

Mergers – Choice of Raider

Name	Make-up of board (no.)	Size (Market Value (£m))	Size (Book Value (£m))
1. Alders (Tamworth) Ltd	4	3·009	2·281
Alliance Box Co. Ltd	3	2·927	1·776
To Form: Alliance Alders Paper and Packaging Ltd			
2. Allen (W. H.) Sons and Co. Ltd	6	6·691	8·513
Bellis and Morcom Ltd	5	4·366	4·577
To Form: Amalgamated Power Eng. Ltd			
3. Algrey Holdings Ltd	5	98·952	0·744
Leeds Fireclay Ltd	0	0·722	0·883
To Form: Leeds Assets Ltd			
4. Allied Land and Investment Co. Ltd	6	11·231	9·534
Lambton Close Holdings Ltd	2	1·486	2·874
To Form: Allied Land Holdings Ltd			
5. Ind Coope Ltd	8	119·277	58·884
Ansells Brewery Ltd	4	55·312	18·936
Tetley Walker Ltd	5	*	*
To Form: Allied Breweries Ltd			
6. Elliott Bros. (London) Ltd	8	1·910	2·405
Associated Automation Ltd	3	3·682	2·193
To Form: Elliott–Automation Ltd			
7. Balfour (Arthur) and Co. Ltd	7	2·856	3·055
Darwins Group Ltd	3	4·053	2·864
To Form: Balfour and Darwins Ltd			
8. Barfos Ltd	6	2·112	1·827
Dawson Bros. Ltd	4	1·636	1·188
To Form: Dawson and Barfos Ltd			
9. Charrington Utd Breweries Ltd	7	217·274	139·278
Bass, Mitchells and Butlers Ltd	8	146·610	81·905
To Form: Bass Charrington Ltd			
10. Mitchells and Butlers Ltd	7	59·627	27·103
Bass Ratcliff and Gretton Ltd	3	54·949	26·342
To Form: Bass, Mitchells & Butlers Ltd			

TABLE III – *cont.*

Name	Make-up of board (no.)	Size (Market Value ($£m$))	Size (Book Value ($£m$))
11. Bell and Nicholson Ltd	6	3·018	4·867
Lunt (Richard) Ltd	3	0·771	1·131
To Form: Bell Nicholson & R. Lunt Ltd			
12. Block and Anderson Ltd	6	3·955	1·197
Kolok Mfg Co. Ltd	3	1·458	0·741
To Form: Block Anderson & Kolok Ltd			
13. Charington and Co Ltd	8	40·214	35·060
United Breweries Ltd	5	64·259	40·162
To Form: Charrington Utd Breweries Ltd			
14. Taylor Turncliffe (Elect. Engrg) Ltd	7	3·152	1·827
Bullers Ltd	5	1·207	1·551
To Form: Allied Insulators Ltd			
15. Bury Felt Mfg Co. Ltd	7	1·491	1·672
Mitchells Ashworth & Stansfield Ltd	4	0·956	1·399
To Form: Bury Masco Ltd			
16. Foulkes (A. D.) Ltd	7	1·559	1·023
Cleaver (A. R. & W.) Ltd	4	1·593	1·406
To Form: Mercian Builders Merchants Ltd			
17. Coats (J. P.) Ltd	10	105·413	72·900
Patons and Baldwins Ltd	5	45·036	30·033
To Form: Coats Patons Ltd			
18. Pye Ltd	5	21·833	16·925
Cole (E. K.) Ltd	3	12·621	7·640
To Form: British Electronic Inds Ltd			
19. United Dairies Ltd	9	22·612	18·384
Cow and Gate Ltd	6	14·878	11·212
To Form: Unigate Ltd			
20. Crittall Mfg Co. Ltd	5	9·806	8·642
Hope (Henry) Ltd	6	5·832	8·180
To Form: Crittall–Hope Ltd			
21. Daily Mirror Newspapers Ltd	9	150·903	64·406
Sunday Pictorial Newspapers Ltd	6	9·769	8·754
To Form: International Publishing Co. Ltd			

TABLE III – *cont.*

Name	Make-up of board (no.)	Size (Market Value (£m))	Size (Book Value (£m))
22. Devon Trading Co. Ltd	4	2·285	1·550
Harvey and Co. Ltd	5	1·931	1·360
To Form: Devon Trading and Harveys Ltd			
23. Metal Agencies Co. Ltd	6	7·482	2·551
Dibben (William) and Son Ltd	2	2·834	2·113
To Form: United Builders Merchants Ltd			
24. Dickinson (John) Ltd	6	73·596	22·764
Robinson (E. S. & A.) Ltd	5	69·384	43·311
To Form: Dickinson Robinson Group Ltd			
25. Dobson Hardwick Ltd	9	12·308	5·497
Park (Wm.) & Co. (Forgemasters) Ltd	6	11·249	6·567
To Form: Dobson Park Industries Ltd			
26. Dufay Ltd	7	3·296	0·501
Wailes Dove Bitumastic Ltd	0	2·000	1·130
To Form: Dufay Bitumastic Ltd			
27. Hackbridge & Hewitt Electric Co. Ltd	8	3·825	2·311
Switchgear & Cowans Ltd	8	1·534	0·961
To Form: Combined Electrical Mfrs Ltd			
28. Hall and Co. Ltd	10	8·530	4·459
Thames Grit and Aggregates Ltd	3	2·931	2·047
To Form: Hall & Ham River Ltd			
29. Hammonds United Breweries Ltd	6	15·936	10·189
Hope & Anchor Breweries Ltd	3	2·796	3·062
Jeffrey (John) & Co. Ltd	0	0·887	1·262
To Form: United Breweries Ltd			
30. Holloway's Properties Ltd	7	4·903	8·255
Sackville Estates Ltd	4	2·038	2·823
To Form: Holloway Sackville Props Ltd			
31. Leyland Motor Corp. Ltd	9	284·661	158·145
British Motor Holdings Ltd	4	310·159	183·526
To Form: British Leyland Motor Corp. Ltd			
32. Redfern (Holdings) Ltd	8	1·005	0·990
Miles (H. G.) (Holdings) Ltd	4	1·449	1·108
To Form: Miles Redfern Ltd			

TABLE III – *cont.*

Name	Make-up of board (no.)	Size (Market Value (£m))	Size (Book Value (£m))
33. Paul (R. & W.) Ltd	7	5·330	4·750
White, Tomkins and Courage Ltd	5	3·890	2·526
To Form: Pauls & Whites Ltd			
34. Pratt (J. Alfred) & Co. (1928) Ltd	7	1·492	0·699
Standard Range & Foundry Ltd	4	1·052	0·650
To Form: Pratt Standard Range Ltd			
35. Vine Products Ltd	5	10·725	4·733
Showerings Ltd	4	9·420	4·799
Whiteways Cider Co. Ltd	2	2·075	1·316
To Form: Showerings, Vine Prods & Whit. Ltd			
36. Wadham Holdings Ltd	9	6·221	5·414
Stringer Motors Ltd	6	3·866	3·032
To Form: Wadham Stringer Ltd			
37. Tetley (Joshua) & Son Ltd	6	35·753	15·890
Walker Cain Ltd	4	18·578	14·934
To Form: Tetley Walker Ltd			
38. Albion Securities Ltd	8	1·557	1·759
Bank & Commercial Premises Trust Ltd	4	†	†
To Form: Bank & Commercial Holdings Ltd.			
39. Liverpool Central Oil Co. Ltd	5	0·173	0·085
Radcliffe's Edible Products Ltd	2	†	†

* Not available – no accounts made up.
† Not available as not public quoted company.

made it possible to classify those companies for which the make-up of the new board proved inconclusive in classifying the companies.

C   Time Period

Annual Data was collected for all 3566 companies in the final population for a thirteen year period 1957–69 inclusive, with the following exceptions:

1. Data for companies which have gone public or had their voting shares first quoted as from a year since 1957 are excluded prior to the quotation of the shares,
2. Companies which were taken over or merged within the census period have a minimum of three years' observations prior to the bid but none after the takeover. That is, for a company taken over between 1957 and 1960, the observations three years prior to the bid has been collected. For a company taken over after 1960, data have been collected for all years between 1957 and the offer.

D   Companies Which Have Gone Public Or Were First Quoted After 1957

It is a normal practice for newly public companies to have their voting capital quoted on a stock exchange within several months of going public. If the granting of their quotation occurs in the second half of the year, that set of annual observations has been omitted on the grounds that the shares have not had sufficient exposure to the market and that the balance sheet data refers predominantly to a period in which the company was privately controlled. If the quotation was granted between January and June, the observations are retained. A parallel practice is employed with companies which first received a quotation after 1957 or whose shares have been reintroduced after the quotation had been suspended for more than a year.

Similarly, companies whose activities were outside the industrial – commercial population described in section I above, but which changed to an activity included within the population definition, have been collected only after that change. Typically these companies were previously involved in tea or rubber plantations and their estates were sold in the late 1950s. Such companies often retained their quotation and this shell was used as a vehicle for different management to absorb companies in another line of business.

E   Company Reorganisation and Change of Name

The identification of takeovers and the collection of data was made more difficult because a number of companies changed their name during the time period. Most changes of name fall into the following categories:

1. Change to a holding company – e.g. Fordham Pressings Ltd to Fordham Holdings Ltd
2. Shortening of the name – e.g. British Plaster Board Holdings Ltd to BPB Industries Ltd
3. Change in the nature of business – e.g. Bowlona Tea Estates Ltd to Grampian Holdings Ltd
4. Change following a takeover – e.g. Amalgamated Cotton Mills Trust Ltd to British Van Heusen Corp. Ltd when it took over British Van Heusen Co Ltd.

When a company reorganises itself it is either to alter the character of its share capital or to change the company to a holding company. In such cases, a new company is formed to acquire the capital of the old one and there is no change in management or control. For the purposes of this study, company reorganisation is treated as a change of name and consequently ignored, excepting as it affects the number and nominal value of the voting equity.

F   Accounting Practices and Accounting Year End

Accounting practices vary from company to company on such items as depreciation rates, definitions of profits and the valuation of assets. In addition to the standardisation of accounting techniques required for tax purposes and the minimum disclosure requirements of the Companies Acts, EXTEL have made comparable (in so far as is possible) the financial variables which are examined in this study. Specifically, companies supply their accounts to varying levels of breakdown and detail so that a column of data supplied by EXTEL for (for example) profits after tax has the same components as the other companies for this variable.

The accounting year is always a period of twelve months except when there is a change in the date on which the company closes its books. In many cases, however, it does not correspond to the calendar year. Any system of adjustment which attempts to relate all firm's accounts to the calendar year is arbitrary by necessity. It was decided that for companies whose accounting year does not end on 3 December, their financial data would be counted as referring to that year in which a majority of their business activity occurs. That is, a company whose accounting year ends on 30 September is treated as if it ended three months later on 31 December, whereas an accounting year ending on 31 March is treated as if it ended three months earlier on the previous 31 December. For accounting years ending 30 June it was decided to have the financial data refer to the current year end (i.e. a 30 June, 1965 ending refers to the year 1965). A difficulty arises when companies change their accounting year end so that under the above system there are no annual observations available (e.g. a change from 31 March to 30 September whereby the accounts are made up for an eighteen month period). Rather than regard accounting years ending in March for such companies as if they ended on 31 December of the same year, the resulting blank year was made up by averaging a twelve month level for the previous and following years for the relevant variables.

G Definitions of the Annual Data Collected

All the following data have been collected annually for each firm and recorded on magnetic computer tape:

1. *Share Prices* – Both the annual high and low share price for each year has been collected for the voting shares of each company. For several companies no markings were recorded in particular years. Where this was so, the average high share price for the preceding and following year was placed as the high for the missing year. Similarly, for the low share price the average of the preceding and following year's low was inserted. Share prices have been adjusted to reflect any changes in the number of issued shares during that year. The figure used is accurate to the nearest old half-penny.

2. *Net Assets Per Share* – This figure is defined as the book value of the company divided by the number of issued voting shares. It has been adjusted in the same way as share prices for changes in the number of issued shares so that it corresponds to the calendar year. The accuracy here is to the nearest old half-penny.

3. *Net Assets (Size)* – This is the book value of the company defined as fixed assets net of depreciation plus current

assets minus current liabilities. Intangibles including goodwill have been excluded. Accuracy is to the nearest £1000.

4. *Net Profits Before Interest Payments and Tax* – This is defined as profits net of depreciation and amortisation and directors emoluments but taken before debenture interest, bank and loan interest, preference dividends and tax have been subtracted. Accuracy is to the nearest £1000.

5. *Net Profits After Tax* – This figure is equal to (4 above) minus payments for tax, interest and minority interest. Accuracy is to the nearest £1000.

6. *Retained Profits* – This is equal to net profits after tax (5 above) minus preference and ordinary dividends and is accurate to the nearest £1000.

7. *Depreciation plus Amortisation* – This is the amount allocated to costs by the firm for capital consumption and will depend on the life expectancy of the company's capital stock. For property companies (where a figure for amortisation is applicable by the nature of their business) the company accounts lump depreciation and amortisation together so that this was by necessity the figure collected. It was not unusual to find a company changing its methods of depreciation during the time period examined. Accuracy of the annual figure is to the nearest £1000.

8. *Liquidity* – This is defined as cash, tax reserve certificates and marketable securities minus bank overdrafts and short term loans, dividend and interest liabilities and current tax liabilities. Accuracy again is to the nearest £1000.

The above nine rows of data, collected for each firm for each available year, have been punched onto cards and stored on magnetic tape for use in the statistical analysis in this study. In addition, there are seven further rows of data on magnetic tape for each firm. These are as follows:

1. Annual valuation ratios with the low share price in the numerator

2. Annual valuation ratios using the median share price (average of the annual high and low) in the numerator

3. Annual ratios of profits before tax divided by the opening size (net assets) of the company (i.e. the ratio of profits

earned \throughout the year divided by the capital available at the beginning of the year)

4. Annual ratios of liquid assets to the closing size of the company (i.e. the ratio of liquid assets at the end of the accounting year to the total net assets at the end of the accounting year)
5. Annual ratios of profits after tax to opening size of the firm
6. Annual ratios of retained profits to profits after tax
7. Annual cash flow which is the sum of depreciation plus net profits after tax divided by the opening size of the firm.

Thus for each firm there exists on magnetic tape sixteen rows of annual data.

H Error Detection

Errors in the data may have crept in at several stages of collection. Assuming the published company accounts are accurate and that EXTEL was able to reproduce these without error, there remains two stages at which errors could have occurred; the extraction of data from EXTEL cards to the 8×5 in. company cards and the punching of the data from these cards. Errors which might have emerged in the compiling stage have been minimised in the following way. First, data for companies taken over were double-checked for the three years prior to the offer. Second, as it required one and one-half years to collect the data, the latest observations needed to be added as they became available. When this was done, the figure for the previous year was checked thereby removing any possibility of an erroneous transposition of rows. Consequently errors that do remain are either a wrong decimal point or a wrong digit. Decimal point placement was checked at the programming stage since all figures in each row were carried out to the same degree of accuracy. A wrong digit still might occur in the data but major errors have been minimised by checking in the program that for each year the following relationships hold:

1. Size > Pre-tax Profits > Profits After Tax > Retentions
2. Size > Depreciation
3. Size > Liquidity

Also, if the above relationships hold, any errors are likely to be relatively small and, as all data except for three years prior to a takeover (which was double-checked) will be averaged over a number of years before being used in statistical analysis, the effect of a numerical error will be diminished. With regard to punching errors, these were avoided by independently punching all data twice and only accepting the punched cards for entry onto the magnetic tape where the two agreed.

I Additional Data Collected For Each Company

1. *Industrial Classifications* – All firms have been classified as belonging to one or more industry groups. Sixty-seven industry classifications have been derived essentially from the *Stock Exchange Official Year Book*. In some cases small classes have been grouped and very large classes have been subdivided if a natural subdivision existed. Changes have also been made in classifying a company if there was a sufficient change in the nature of its business so as to totally change its industry group. Expansion of companies' activities into new industries has been included as successive volumes of the Year Book were examined and changes in the industry classes of each firm noted. Table IV below gives the percentage number of firms belonging to one and more industry classes and table V gives the full description of each of the 67 industry classes.

2. *Accounting Year End* – The month in which the accounting year of the company ends is included as data in the form of a decimal (i.e. December as 0·00, March as 0·75, June as 0·50, and so forth). Almost without exception, the accounts are made up to the last day of the month in which the year ends. When there are changes in the accounting year end, the decimal chosen refers either to the most often occurring year end or, if there are an equal number of years ending in, for example, September and December, the most recent is chosen. If a firm is taken over, the decimal always refers to the latest accounting year end prior to the takeover. Table

VI below gives the percentage distribution of accounting year endings by month.

3. *Date On Which the Company Went Public* – This is given as a continuous variable counting backward from 31 December, 1970 which is set at 0·00. That is, if a firm went public in June 1965, the figure used would be 5·50 as June 1965 is five and one-half years prior to December 1970. Similarly, if a firm went public in September 1931, the figure used is 39·25. For companies which went public prior to 1930, only the year is available and not the month so that a company which went public in 1901 is given 69·00. Thus by this transformation, a variable is available for the age of each company.

4. *Company Identification* – The name of each company does not appear on the magnetic tape input. A company may however be identified by a code letter and number which appears with the other input data.

J Additional Information Collected For Companies Taken Over

1. *Identification of Raider* – Raiders' identification codes are given if the raider is among the population of firms involved in this study. The following means of classification of raiders outside the population is used. Table VII presents the nine alternative classifications of raiders outside the population and the number of raiders in each class.

TABLE IV

No. of industry classes	% of companies with each number
1	47·61
2	23·47
3	12·88
4	7·21
5	4·72
6	2·37
7	1·40
8	0·20
9	0·03

TABLE V

Description of Industrial Classifications

Industry no.	Description
1.	Agricultural & Dairy Machinery & Equipment
2.	Aircraft & Aero Engines, Accessories & Components
3.	Asbestos, Asphalte, Bitumen & Tar
4.	Bricks, Tiles, Fireclay, Cement, Concrete & Concrete Products, Refactories
5.	Builders & Contractors, Decorators & Shopfitters, Prefabricated Buildings
6.	Builders' Merchants, Building Materials, Timber, Plant Hire
7.	Cable Manufacturers, Rope, Twine, Belting, Nettings, Wire & Wire Ropes
8.	Engineers – Civil & Constructional, Public Works Contractors
9.	Engineers – Electrical & Electronics
10.	Engineers – General
11.	Engineers – Marine, Mining, Railway
12.	Engineers – Metal Manufacturers & Refining, Founders, Forgers, Galvanising
13.	Engineers – Textile Machinery
14.	Engineers – Heating, Lighting, Cooking, Ventilating
15.	Ironfounders & Engineers, Steel Manufacturers
16.	Machine Tools, Small Tools, Instruments & Sundries
17.	Miscellaneous Machinery, Plant & Boiler Makers
18.	Refrigeration, Coldstores, Ice
19.	Shipbuilders & Repairers, Shipbreakers, Canals & Docks
20.	Carpets, Rugs, Felt, Linoleum, Floorcloth
21.	China, Glass, Pottery
22.	Furnishers, Furniture Makers & Furniture Stores
23.	Hardware & Ironmongery
24.	Motor Vehicle & Cycle Manufacturers
25.	Motor Vehicle & Cycle Accessories & Components
26.	Motor Vehicle & Cycle Dealers & Repairers, Garage Proprietors
27.	Office Equipment
28.	Paints, Polishes, Varnishes, Enamels, Printing Inks
29.	Plastics & Plastic Goods
30.	Radio & Television, Musical Instruments, Records, Photographic Equipment & Film Production
31.	Rubber Products
32.	Leather & Leather Goods
33.	Toys, Perambulators, Sports Goods, Nursery Equipment
34.	Timber, Plywood, Veneer Cutters, Woodworkers
35.	Animal Feeding Stuffs, Millers, Grain Merchants, Seed Merchants, Nurserymen
36.	Breweries & Distilleries, Malters, Wines, Spirits & Beers, Bottlers

TABLE V

Industry no.	Description
37.	Boots & Shoes
38.	Clothing Manufacturers & Merchants
39.	Containers & Packing Material
40.	Entertainments – Cinemas, Concert Halls, Exhibitions, Greyhounds, Racecourses, Sports Arenas, Holiday Camps, Piers, Theatres
41.	Food, Bakers, Confectioners, Dairy Products, Butchers, Grocers, Fruit, Patent Foods, Canners
42.	Hotels, Caterers, Restaurants
43.	Medical, Dental, Optical & Surgical Equipment
44.	Mineral Waters, Soft Drinks, Cider, Cordials
45.	Newspapers, Periodicals
46.	Paper & Pulp, Paper Goods, Wallpapers
47.	Printers, Bookbinders, Publishers, Stationers, Advertising Agents
48.	Chemists & Druggists, Soap, Candles, Perfumery, Toilet Articles
49.	Stores – Departmental & Mail Order
50.	Stores – Drapers, Glovers, Hatters, Milliners, Furriers, Outfitters, Tailors
51.	Stores – General Merchants, Warehousemen, Importers & Exporters
52.	Stores – Jewellers, Cutlers, Silver, Clocks, Watches
53.	Textiles – Cotton
54.	Textiles – General, Bleachers & Dyers, Wholesalers & Distribution
55.	Textiles – Hosiery & Underwear
56.	Textiles – Rayon, Nylon & Artificial Fabrics
57.	Textiles – Wool, Worsted, Woollen Goods
58.	Tobacco, Matches, Smokers' Requisites
59.	Financial Trusts, Finance, Hire Purchase & Mortgage Companies
60.	Insurance Brokers
61.	Property Companies, Markets, Exchanges, Office Buildings
62.	Chemicals
63.	Laundries, Dyers & Cleaners
64.	Oil Production, Refining & Distribution
65.	Shipping Companies, Tankers, Trawlers, Whalers
66.	Wharves & Warehouses
67.	Tramways, Omnibus, Road Haulage Contractors

TABLE VI

Monthly Distribution of Accounting Year Ends

Month	% of companies with accounting years ending
January	4·50
February	2·21
March	25·29
April	3·24
May	1·51
June	7·82
July	3·69
August	1·76
September	11·18
October	3·16
November	1·87
December	33·53

TABLE VII

Classes and Distribution of Raiders Outside Population

Classification	No. of raiders in each
1. Raiders which have gone into liquidation after the takeover	18
2. American companies as raiders	47
3. Other foreign companies as raiders	12
4. Non-quoted companies as raiders	128
5. Raiders too new to be in population	18
6. Investment trusts or banks as raiders	18
7. Commodity group raiders such as mining and plantations	11
8. Private individual(s) as raiders	20
9. Raiders which have been nationalised	1

2. *Industrial Classes of Raiders* – These are available on the computer input tape for raiders within the census population in the data block of the acquired firms.

3. *Takeover Date* – This is given a value in the same way as the date the firm went public (section I.3 above). Thus a company taken over in June 1957 is given 13.50. Subtracting this number from the number associated with the date the firm went public yields a new variable for the age of the company when it was taken over. Normally several months are required to finalise a bid (though there have been instances of offers requiring a year or more to be declared unconditional), so the date given is that of the first mention of a bid. This means that a successful offer made at the end of 1956 but not declared unconditional until early 1957 is not included.

4. *Offer Terms* – Details of the way in which the takeover was paid for are given by having the conditions of the offer fall into one of the following five categories:
   a. Cash including market purchases and payment by debenture stock
   b. Cash plus shares; cash plus convertible unsecured loan stock; cash plus shares plus convertible loan stock
   c. Share exchange
   d. Convertible loan stock or shares plus convertible loan stock
   e. Sale by the raider of one of its subsidiaries to the acquired firm which issues its voting shares as payment thereby giving the raider voting control

5. *Pre- and Post-Offer Share Prices* – The share price before any mention of a bid and the share price after the final bid has been made, has been collected for each firm taken over.

6. *Unsuccessful Raids* – In addition to the collection of the details (in sections J.1 to J.5 above) for successful takeovers, the same information has been gathered for unsuccessful attempts at takeover. It was, however, only possible to compile a complete list of these since the beginning of 1966.

Appendix II:

Supporting Data

TABLE Ia

Monthly Distribution of Takeovers – 1957–69

Year	Jan	Feb	Mar	Apr	May	Jun	Jul	Aug	Sep	Oct	Nov	Dec	Row total
1957	6	8	4	5	4	5	15	4	6	4	11	4	76
1958	6	5	3	4	4	2	8	8	8	11	10	14	83
1959	8	11	11	14	16	14	14	7	3	10	16	14	138
1960	5	13	8	6	7	7	10	13	8	15	4	11	107
1961	10	14	8	6	11	9	8	5	8	8	12	14	113
1962	7	9	6	8	7	8	8	9	7	14	6	9	98
1963	4	9	7	9	7	3	8	3	7	12	10	11	90
1964	8	13	3	4	8	14	16	13	6	9	6	12	112
1965	5	12	10	14	4	8	5	6	9	3	9	15	100
1966	7	11	10	4	7	3	14	8	2	6	9	8	89
1967	6	6	12	8	17	18	9	18	15	9	17	9	144
1968	15	18	17	14	20	15	28	24	15	24	23	27	240
1969	23	19	13	13	11	6	14	9	17	12	13	14	164
													1554

TABLE Ib

Monthly Value of Takeovers (Net Assets) – 1957–69 (£m)

Year	Jan	Feb	Mar	Apr	May	Jun	Jul	Aug	Sep	Oct	Nov	Dec	Row total
1957	2·423	13·748	3·216	49·799	2·326	6·336	17·939	6·456	4·884	5·392	9·171	5·783	127·509
1958	4·811	4·840	1·742	6·076	4·706	1·883	16·666	8·811	6·392	26·195	29·713	82·446	194·281
1959	21·887	12·141	12·031	23·432	22·868	41·822	20·620	7·318	1·020	10·296	12·339	67·406	253·180
1960	17·335	24·152	16·491	19·434	34·476	15·194	19·700	29·518	12·647	36·842	10·076	62·690	298·555
1961	23·466	49·719	37·707	21·429	41·182	20·265	11·018	26·074	12·642	28·011	27·520	36·139	335·172
1962	30·316	7·596	5·865	73·970	13·239	14·622	10·141	28·570	9·113	38·113	5·255	7·860	244·660
1963	2·177	19·762	9·270	20·143	19·634	4·676	30·360	2·595	8·414	22·771	40·052	36·242	216·096
1964	9·240	32·345	11·218	5·218	13·759	22·260	58·823	67·267	13·404	28·571	16·261	11·117	290·032
1965	7·334	47·705	90·694	33·332	35·491	13·721	3·142	100·004	32·224	5·318	59·550	38·067	466·582
1966	26·883	31·077	17·798	53·141	24·410	25·623	64·790	43·856	3·360	7·559	52·454	35·710	386·832
1967	138·194	38·336	46·256	94·852	54·804	118·047	111·204	61·090	30·637	237·996	70·662	59·014	1060·992
1968	349·141	88·134	90·775	92·974	92·483	32·891	251·772	99·543	422·068	160·099	179·838	100·802	1960·520
1969	333·238	69·444	74·026	36·682	75·461	20·578	56·123	69·743	56·016	38·098	125·387	48·648	1003·444
													6837·855

TABLE Ic

Monthly Market Value of Takeovers 1957–69 (£m)

Year	Jan	Feb	Mar	Apr	May	Jun	Jul	Aug	Sep	Oct	Nov	Dec	Row total
1957	1·689	19·951	3·544	28·451	2·960	4·382	25·996	5·112	5·203	5·497	10·321	4·460	117·556
1958	4·255	3·641	1·549	5·009	6·488	1·764	14·408	12·635	7·479	19·809	27·358	86·301	190·696
1959	24·443	10·015	21·229	28·385	27·551	71·640	33·095	10·251	0·956	33·606	21·173	80·912	363·256
1960	35·010	33·526	41·073	19·925	58·515	19·013	42·644	60·695	26·908	44·341	16·616	75·693	473·959
1961	56·474	132·472	45·729	62·121	97·804	36·019	25·481	34·560	27·275	33·198	39·820	87·711	678·711
1962	50·013	17·379	14·069	126·925	18·594	30·207	14·245	34·447	17·876	55·802	6·567	15·521	399·645
1963	3·992	34·631	18·745	22·554	30·860	9·425	69·507	3·108	18·638	58·465	63·192	59·669	392·768
1964	20·042	43·636	19·787	5·810	26·660	43·023	107·599	74·988	28·162	36·895	20·223	11·516	438·341
1965	13·900	73·377	144·107	81·449	15·767	21·034	5·309	93·903	76·596	7·227	104·396	73·331	710·396
1966	37·634	57·146	19·205	75·420	28·747	28·623	110·228	57·777	4·649	10·185	89·616	47·641	566·871
1967	180·992	48·332	168·197	148·658	83·401	191·175	224·141	116·046	32·353	269·938	110·358	127·973	1701·564
1968	995·784	147·710	109·792	164·155	220·446	62·147	800·428	246·708	906·025	499·223	410·996	189·139	4752·553
1969	903·507	113·535	153·677	70·378	138·777	33·815	173·312	214·840	194·339	70·758	218·271	82·902	2368·111

13154·398

TABLE Id

Extel Security Values Index Dec 1956 = 100 – 1957–69 Calculated on Mid-month Prices of 176 Variable Dividend Securities

Year	Jan	Feb	Mar	Apr	May	Jun	Jul	Aug	Sep	Oct	Nov	Dec	Row total/12
1957	104·0	106·5	106·0	112·0	116·0	117·0	117·5	115·5	110·0	97·0	95·0	96·0	107·7
1958	93·0	91·5	93·0	96·5	96·5	101·5	101·5	107·5	112·0	118·5	121·0	123·0	104·6
1959	129·5	129·5	130·5	133·5	141·0	145·5	144·0	149·0	154·0	165·0	178·0	182·0	148·4
1960	191·0	185·0	174·5	177·5	172·0	178·5	175·0	184·0	185·5	185·5	185·5	177·0	180·9
1961	186·0	190·0	198·5	206·5	218·5	204·0	187·0	190·0	186·5	183·0	194·5	193·5	194·8
1962	197·5	197·5	195·5	202·0	205·5	182·5	181·0	193·5	188·5	190·0	197·0	198·0	194·0
1963	197·0	200·0	205·0	206·0	208·0	205·0	209·0	213·5	215·0	217·5	220·5	223·5	210·0
1964	218·5	217·0	221·5	227·0	222·5	220·5	228·0	231·0	228·5	227·0	222·0	211·5	222·9
1965	214·5	220·0	210·5	210·0	219·5	212·0	206·0	211·5	213·0	221·5	224·0	222·5	215·4
1966	227·0	236·5	228·5	229·0	238·0	239·0	236·0	212·0	207·0	204·0	199·5	205·0	221·8
1967	212·5	213·0	214·0	225·0	229·5	230·0	234·0	235·0	244·0	255·0	273·0	279·5	237·0
1968	278·5	294·5	293·0	316·5	330·0	346·0	361·0	365·0	373·0	362·5	372·0	385·5	339·8
1969	402·0	396·5	372·5	365·0	347·0	310·0	295·0	294·0	299·0	304·0	300·0	301·5	332·2

TABLE IIa

Mean Values of Industry Performance

Ind.	Profit Rate	Growth Rate	Retention Ratio	Liquidity Ratio	Valuation ratio	Size
1	0·16511	0·33827	0·43457	−0·12559	1·10618	3·93688
2	0·17891	0·50635	0·50047	−0·06638	1·21501	11·20502
3	0·22077	0·57064	0·46728	−0·05541	1·70234	4·62229
4	0·17804	0·38924	0·43267	−0·05138	1·36460	4·19586
5	0·22605	0·54906	0·73539	−0·16123	2·43713	3·68776
6	0·18139	0·22653	0·43712	−0·13449	2·19641	4·08901
7	0·16371	0·13202	0·44972	−0·00479	1·07800	13·86076
8	0·18746	0·35662	0·71426	−0·10198	2·61389	4·08254
9	0·20277	0·29364	0·51317	−0·06054	2·45183	8·18898
10	0·18301	0·36176	0·45409	−0·06832	1·87616	6·86178
11	0·15299	0·16443	0·43961	−0·01805	1·12276	7·93655
12	0·17957	0·30993	0·41557	−0·04176	1·44265	6·03485
13	0·19107	0·18694	0·44245	−0·02942	1·34193	6·16152
14	0·29513	0·20282	0·63978	−0·05853	1·46503	5·44537
15	0·17405	0·15432	0·44997	−0·03213	1·12373	10·33107
16	0·18857	0·28106	0·43697	−0·04736	1·27832	4·04924
17	0·17840	0·18986	0·58441	−0·01983	1·40713	5·30835
18	0·24318	0·44917	0·47998	−0·06641	2·02754	6·12573
19	0·09375	0·09137	0·51531	−0·08181	0·97945	12·81922
20	0·16694	0·19257	0·45236	−0·09741	1·16068	4·08477
21	0·16704	0·18589	0·45589	−0·02850	1·17499	2·81951
22	0·18717	0·19024	0·43439	−0·10895	1·44747	5·56775
23	0·16619	0·22378	0·10320	−0·09760	1·87400	5·06720
24	0·15985	0·11768	0·51754	−0·09197	1·17298	18·02194
25	0·18722	0·22758	0·48382	−0·05576	1·02990	7·51837
26	0·15904	0·03890	0·43821	−0·21523	1·45775	3·85180
27	0·19677	0·32941	0·45987	−0·03757	1·52232	4·06426
28	0·20041	0·25466	0·39612	−0·05257	1·59525	17·91071
29	0·18765	0·23330	0·47845	−0·07278	1·69425	13·18534
30	0·20105	0·32214	0·50349	−0·11413	1·57112	5·81216
31	0·19053	0·21257	0·42015	−0·06333	1·52465	8·68756
32	0·12944	0·10630	0·44164	−0·06232	1·02033	1·68344
33	0·23633	0·54526	0·39774	−0·08949	2·10113	2·09003
34	0·15770	0·21512	0·41232	−0·15086	1·06569	2·03602
35	0·15365	0·27503	0·36283	−0·07194	1·54832	16·80899
36	0·14820	0·19900	0·43440	−0·03287	1·30680	14·84290
37	0·16697	0·19551	0·43073	−0·07505	1·35909	4·20459
38	0·19910	0·24657	0·42934	−0·08159	1·19565	2·71945
39	0·17320	0·29796	0·40755	−0·04326	1·24739	5·49196
40	0·14580	0·28549	0·31885	−0·10746	3·35608	2·34141
41	0·18629	0·30088	0·42078	−0·04492	2·35917	9·92919

TABLE IIa – *cont.*

Ind.	Profit Rate	Growth Rate	Retention Ratio	Liquidity Ratio	Valuation ratio	Size
42	0·18899	0·66224	0·43132	−0·01080	2·26327	4·27108
43	0·22295	0·22316	0·42938	−0·04622	1·54774	9·90528
44	0·17135	0·18085	0·44234	−0·02397	1·49933	8·35993
45	0·23336	0·24249	0·38458	−0·08085	5·17634	7·56093
46	0·17218	0·23579	0·45810	−0·00680	1·14421	37·63106
47	0·13959	0·15278	0·29033	−0·00417	3·08969	5·02790
48	0·21262	0·22607	0·44162	−0·00283	3·24798	34·86340
49	0·17497	0·22786	0·37770	−0·08767	1·72291	12·11963
50	0·16837	0·08954	0·17164	−0·20147	2·39074	8·87085
51	0·13266	0·16995	0·41200	−0·11614	0·98210	7·58861
52	0·20796	0·21896	0·45471	−0·03819	1·46457	4·97147
53	0·11672	0·09064	0·27827	−0·02531	0·85911	7·43464
54	0·09380	0·11947	0·33701	−0·03043	0·69236	5·86356
55	0·18598	0·23011	0·39958	−0·05439	1·32471	5·79074
56	0·13905	0·16552	0·41265	−0·07525	1·11451	15·23870
57	0·14461	0·13802	0·31656	−0·07289	1·17240	4·57074
58	0·16792	0·05726	0·37938	−0·16944	1·57632	16·57101
59	0·13144	0·58870	0·52692	−0·07481	4·39320	11·64548
60	0·47877	0·97371	0·43848	1·06688	6·58708	4·09584
61	0·10321	0·08641	0·26279	−0·08609	2·37657	5·27804
62	0·19044	0·25358	0·85356	−0·01065	1·71565	27·97367
63	0·15215	0·17616	0·39344	−0·01455	1·10451	4·92182
64	0·19341	0·19909	0·44386	−0·01760	1·15824	134·67148
65	0·08250	0·13915	0·44309	−0·07726	0·82426	15·49784
66	0·14112	0·22648	0·40076	−0·07169	1·47793	3·48627
67	0·19438	0·35961	0·44232	−0·07457	1·38319	6·14598

Note: The profit rate is taken before tax and size is in £m. All other variables are ratios. The valuation ratio is measured as in regression 1 chapter 3.

TABLE IIb

Median Values of Industry Performance

Ind.	Profit Rate	Growth Rate	Retention Ratio	Liquidity Ratio	Valuation ratio	Size
1	0·14671	0·09679	0·43996	−0·13641	0·92513	1·90479
2	0·15902	0·10655	0·50000	−0·09859	1·01062	2·48600
3	0·16979	0·13630	0·48123	−0·07264	1·49652	1·07834
4	0·15837	0·11810	0·42948	−0·05016	1·07716	1·52589
5	0·18550	0·18244	0·48000	−0·17292	1·44983	1·78140
6	0·15987	0·11812	0·46165	−0·14165	1·09492	1·60169
7	0·14486	0·08678	0·47729	−0·05085	0·90577	2·05308
8	0·16449	0·14121	0·50430	−0·12605	1·17572	1·68985
9	0·16862	0·11905	0·50000	−0·09303	1·14873	2·04415
10	0·15940	0·10981	0·46464	−0·08706	1·01650	1·91923
11	0·13469	0·08393	0·47542	−0·06938	0·86231	2·54400
12	0·16190	0·09769	0·46679	−0·06371	0·96643	1·68985
13	0·18294	0·12733	0·49461	−0·09061	1·14375	1·85123
14	0·15373	0·10874	0·47016	−0·08679	1·10731	1·85300
15	0·15508	0·09818	0·47529	−0·04195	0·89996	2·31160
16	0·16563	0·09633	0·46712	−0·07794	1·02609	1·71000
17	0·15972	0·09069	0·47256	−0·06282	0·96380	2·04342
18	0·15373	0·12005	0·48630	−0·11935	1·23733	1·64000
19	0·08816	0·03611	0·50430	0·02851	0·61518	2·90700
20	0·14319	0·08084	0·45833	−0·09503	0·91290	1·53739
21	0·15650	0·11161	0·47120	−0·09091	0·92715	1·47031
22	0·16055	0·08799	0·44703	−0·12569	1·07977	1·10962
23	0·14934	0·09443	0·46224	−0·11907	0·89951	1·40600
24	0·12725	0·11748	0·51910	−0·12960	0·93458	2·69500
25	0·15972	0·11639	0·46464	−0·09105	1·01716	1·60223
26	0·14808	0·15689	0·44668	−0·20500	1·00279	1·47475
27	0·16451	0·11536	0·43860	−0·08654	1·16306	1·62877
28	0·17322	0·11186	0·42669	−0·06729	1·05750	1·50623
29	0·16432	0·12733	0·46108	−0·07794	1·06686	1·23600
30	0·16342	0·10468	0·46515	−0·15392	1·20791	1·64442
31	0·17952	0·08434	0·46165	−0·11226	1·10050	1·82625
32	0·10532	0·04872	0·38129	−0·03903	0·69674	1·01100
33	0·16843	0·10801	0·46601	−0·13988	1·22426	1·26623
34	0·14061	0·08672	0·43041	−0·17353	0·63611	1·36300
35	0·12984	0·09186	0·37500	−0·06587	0·92995	1·00720
36	0·13172	0·08127	0·44559	−0·02806	1·26999	3·17000
37	0·15225	0·09211	0·43975	−0·08189	1·08846	1·17500
38	0·14955	0·09171	0·46891	−0·11226	1·16111	0·96240
39	0·15648	0·10288	0·42746	−0·06581	1·00000	1·58500
40	0·17137	0·06753	0·27050	0·08965	1·56658	0·51100
41	0·15648	0·09187	0·45558	−0·06645	1·06438	1·48408

Table IIb—*cont.*

Ind.	Profit Rate	Growth Rate	Retention Ratio	Liquidity Ratio	Valuation ratio	Size
42	0·14494	0·15220	0·43412	−0·02724	1·36497	1·58792
43	0·17946	0·08492	0·43083	−0·08010	1·21731	2·24100
44	0·17647	0·08440	0·47273	−0·00319	1·01648	2·55300
45	0·22100	0·10426	0·39734	−0·00264	1·34804	2·18154
46	0·14911	0·09023	0·44242	−0·04762	0·98387	2·64377
47	0·19200	0·12492	0·44040	−0·02415	1·14873	1·38700
48	0·18824	0·08862	0·41717	−0·02652	1·44321	1·62000
49	0·14968	0·09697	0·42580	−0·09256	1·18765	1·57400
50	0·18450	0·07523	0·37603	−0·12121	1·08846	1·36585
51	0·10213	0·07443	0·46211	−0·13080	0·75731	2·55623
52	0·18426	0·14590	0·49033	−0·06341	1·27812	0·99417
53	0·08927	0·02372	0·33735	−0·05337	0·65643	1·44700
54	0·10908	0·04349	0·38249	−0·04475	0·73938	1·17500
55	0·16594	0·07392	0·44324	−0·05901	1·00736	1·19800
56	0·11001	0·05724	0·39753	−0·02234	0·73600	1·46100
57	0·13186	0·05314	0·38128	−0·10292	0·85145	1·38062
58	0·18588	0·11907	0·40201	−0·14524	1·23342	1·58580
59	0·11958	0·13689	0·42029	−0·13474	1·20237	2·91915
60	0·41283	0·18664	0·44947	0·75666	4·51429	2·51588
61	0·08627	0·26004	0·18966	−0·07685	1·13022	2·82300
62	0·16757	0·11734	0·40813	−0·01530	1·28400	2·95015
63	0·13532	0·06770	0·43259	0·01753	0·86668	1·08609
64	0·17861	0·10433	0·47368	−0·01160	1·00047	3·40331
65	0·06265	0·05332	0·49333	0·02002	0·53781	4·85185
66	0·11594	0·07472	0·43565	−0·05717	0·85728	2·08200
67	0·13922	0·16923	0·41960	−0·11946	0·94130	1·71308

Note: The profit rate is taken before tax and size is in £m. All other variables are ratios. The valuation ratio is measured as in regression 1 chapter 3.

TABLE III

Ranked Industry Numbers by Proportion of Takeovers; Number of Takeovers; Number of Raiders

Rank	Proportion of takeovers	Number of takeovers	Number of raiders
1	44	41	9
2	36	17	41
3	48	9	10
4	41	54	36
5	55	16	62
6	43	36	61
7	53	61	25
8	50	25	54
9	54	6	53
10	21	12	42
11	42	10	5
12	31	38	16
13	28	14	56
14	66	47	30
15	7	53	48
16	38	56	46
17	35	57	17
18	49	30	14
19	24	8	57
20	3	11	2
21	64	55	7
22	25	2	38
23	51	4	8
24	40	29	26
25	18	23	35
26	39	39	59
27	16	50	11
28	63	48	44
29	56	15	43
30	34	42	65
31	2	34	6
32	57	5	12
33	9	7	47
34	30	51	29
35	17	28	39
36	67	22	50
37	47	62	15
38	6	26	28
39	19	49	49

TABLE – *cont.*

Rank	Proportion of takeover	Number of takeover	Number of raiders
40	61	35	1
41	45	44	55
42	32	40	23
43	14	59	51
44	46	1	24
45	4	46	67
46	1	21	18
47	59	20	4
48	12	43	22
49	11	65	40
50	20	31	21
51	62	3	19
52	29	66	64
53	58	37	52
54	65	24	20
55	22	32	31
56	23	67	3
57	15	19	66
58	33	64	37
59	37	27	27
60	27	45	45
61	26	18	63
62	8	63	33
63	10	33	13
64	52	52	60
65	13	13	34
66	5	58	32
67	60	60	58

Bibliography

Baldwin, W. L. (1964) 'The motives of managers, environmental restraints and the theory of managerial enterprise', *Quarterly Journal of Economics*, 1964.

Baumol, W. J. (1959) *Business Behaviour, Value and Growth*, New York, 1959.

Blood, D. M. and Baker, C. B. (1958) 'Some problems in linear discrimination', *Journal of Farm Economics*, 1958.

Bull, G. and Vice, A. (1958) *Bid for Power*, Elek, 1958.

Cook, P. L. and Cohen, R. (1958) *Effects of Mergers*, London, 1958.

Cowling, K. G., ed. (1972) *Market Structure and Corporate Behaviour: Theory and Empirical Analysis of the Firm*, Grey–Mills, 1972.

Cramer, J. S. (1962) *The Ownership of Major Consumer Durables*, Cambridge, Monograph 7, 1962.

Dewey, D. (1961) 'Mergers and cartels: some reservations about policy', *Market Economic Review*, May 1961.

Dixon, W. J. and Massey, F. J., Jr. (1957) *Introduction to Statistical Analysis*, New York, 1957.

Durand, D. (1941) *Risk Elements in Consumer Instalment Financing*, National Bureau of Economic Research, New York, 1941.

Duvall, R. M. and Austin, D. V. (1965) 'Predicting the results of proxy contests', *Journal of Finance*, 1965.

Eatwell, J. L. (1971) 'Growth, profitability and size: the empirical evidence', *The Corporate Economy*, ed. R. L. Marris and A. Wood, London, 1971.

Encarcion, J. (1964) 'Constraints and the firm's utility function', *Review of Economic Studies*, 1964.

Finney, D. J. (1952) *Probit Analysis*, Cambridge, 1952.

Fisher, R. A. (1944) *Statistical Methods for Research Workers*, 9th ed., Edinburgh, 1944.

—— and Yates, F. (1943) *Statistical Tables for Biological Agricultural and Medical Research*, Edinburgh, 1943.

Goldberger, A. S. (1964) *Econometric Theory*, New York, 1964.

Gort, M. (1969) 'An economic disturbance theory of mergers', *Quarterly Journal of Economics*, Nov. 1969.

Hayes, S. L., III and Taussig, R. A. (1967) 'Tactics of cash takeover bids', *Harvard Business Review*, Mar.–Apr. 1967.

Hindley, B. (1969) 'Capitalism and the corporation', *Economica*, Nov. 1969.

——(1972) 'Recent theory and evidence on corporate merger', *Market Structure and Corporate Behaviour: Theory and Empirical Analysis*, ed. K. G. Cowling, Grey–Mills, 1972.

Johnston, J. (1960) *Statistical Cost Analysis*, New York, 1960.

Kuehn, D. A. (1969) 'Stock market valuation and acquisitions: an empirical test of one component of managerial security', *Journal of Industrial Economics*, Apr. 1969.

——(1972) 'Takeover raiders and the growth maximisation hypothesis', *Market Structure and Corporate Behaviour: Theory and Empirical Analysis*, ed. K. G. Cowling, Grey–Mills, 1972.

—— and Davies, J. R. (1973) 'An empirical analysis of capital market discipline on poor performance and its implications for the theory of the firm', *Proceedings of the 20th International Conference of the Institute of Management Sciences*, Jun. 1973.

Ladd, G. W. (1966) 'Linear probability functions and discriminant functions', *Econometrica*, Oct. 1966.

——(1968) *Analysis of Ranking of Dairy Bargaining Cooperative Objectives*, Iowa Agricultural and Home Economics Experimental Station, 1967–8.

Lee, Maw Lin (1964) 'Income, income change and durable good demand', *Journal of the American Statistical Association*, 1964.

Ma, R. (1960) 'Births and deaths in the quoted public company sector in the United Kingdom, 1949–1953', *Yorkshire Bulletin of Economic and Social Research*, Nov. 1960.

Manne, H. G. (1965) 'Mergers and the market for corporate control', *Journal of Political Economy*, Apr. 1965.

Markham, J. W. (1955) 'Survey of the evidence and findings on mergers', *Business Concentration and Price Policy*, Conference of the Universities – National Bureau Committee for Economic Research, Princeton, 1955.

Marris, R. L. (1963) 'A model of managerial enterprise', *Quarterly Journal of Economics*, 1963.

——(1964) *The Economic Theory of Managerial Capitalism*, London, 1964.

——(1968) 'Galbraith, Solow and the truth about corporations', *The Public Interest*, Spring 1968.

—— and Wood, A. (1971) *The Corporate Economy*, London, 1971.

Mather, K. (1965) *Statistical Analysis in Biology*, London, 1965.

Mennel, W. (1962) *Takeover: The Growth of Monopoly in Britain, 1951–61*, London, 1962.

Moon, R. W. (1968) *Business Mergers and Takeover Bids*, 3rd ed., London, 1968.

Mueller, D. C. (1969) 'A theory of conglomerate merger', *Quarterly Journal of Economics*, Nov. 1969.

Nelson, R. L. (1959) *Merger Movements in American Industry, 1895–1956*, Princeton, 1959.

——(1966) 'Business cycle factors in the choice between internal and external growth', *The Corporate Merger*, ed. J. E. Segall and W. W. Alberts, Chicago, 1966.

Newbould, G. D. (1970) *Management and Merger Activity*, Liverpool, 1970.

Orcutt, G. H., Greenberger, M., Korbel, J. and Rivlin, A. M. (1961) *Microanalysis of Socioeconomic Systems: A Simulation Study*, New York, 1961.

Penrose, E. (1959) *The Theory of the Growth of the Firm*, Oxford, 1959.

Puckett, M. and Friend, O. (1964) 'Dividends and stock prices', *American Economic Review*, Sept. 1964.

Reid, S. R. (1968) *Mergers, Managers and the Economy*, New York, 1968.

Segall, J. E. and Alberts, W. W., eds. (1966) *The Corporate Merger*, Chicago, 1966.

Singh, A. and Whittington, G. (1968) *Growth, Profitability and Valuation*, Cambridge, 1968.

Singh, A. (1971) *Takeovers*, Cambridge, 1971.

Stacey, N. A. N. (1966) *Mergers in Modern Business*, London, 1966.

Tintner, G. (1952) *Econometrics*, New York, 1952.

Warner, S. L. (1962) *Stochastic Choice of Mode of Urban Travel: A Study in Binary Choice*, Chicago, 1962.

Williamson, O. E. (1964) *The Economics of Discretionary Behaviour: Managerial Objectives in a Theory of the Firm*, Englewood Cliffs, 1964.

Index

187